Practica for your old PC

C000246722

by

Ian Sinclair

BERNARD BABANI (publishing) LTD
THE GRAMPIANS
SHEPHERDS BUSH ROAD
LONDON W6 7NF
ENGLAND

PLEASE NOTE

Although every care has been taken with the production of this book to ensure that any projects, designs, modifications and/or programs, etc., contained herewith, operate in a correct and safe manner and also that any components specified are normally available in Great Britain, the Publishers and Author(s) do not accept responsibility in any way for the failure (including fault in design) of any project, design, modification or program to work correctly or to cause damage to any equipment that it may be connected to or used in conjunction with, or in respect of any other damage or injury that may be so caused, nor do the Publishers accept responsibility in any way for the failure to obtain specified components.

Notice is also given that if equipment that is still under warranty is modified in any way or used or connected with home-built equipment then that warranty may be void.

© 1998 BERNARD BABANI (publishing) LTD

First Published –April 1998

British Library Cataloguing in Publication Data:

A catalogue record for this book is available from the British Library

ISBN 0 85934 449 5

Cover Design by Gregor Arthur
Cover Illustration by Adam Willis
Printed and Bound in Great Britain by Cox & Wyman Ltd., Reading

ABOUT THIS BOOK

Every month or so, you find that a computer upgrade either offers more or costs less, or even both. Your old computer seems to have little or no value, and a trade-in is not an option. What, exactly, can you do with an old PC computer? This book answers this question in a positive way, showing that the old computer can be of much more value than its selling price might indicate.

Old is not an absolute terms in PC computing, and though we could all agree that a 1981 PC is an old machine, it requires some gritting of the teeth to admit that the up-to-date computer that you bought last year is now an old computer compared to the faster and more fashionable computer of today (or the better and cheaper one that will be available tomorrow).

On the other hand, if your PC does exactly what you need, and anything more modern would simply add frills that you don't need or want, how can the word 'old' apply to it? *Old* is not a matter of age in years, but of usefulness, and in that sense an elderly machine can be as up to date as you need, and a new one quite irrelevant to your needs.

All of this leads up to the point that when you buy a new computer, there may still be a lot of life in the one that you are replacing. This book makes some suggestions that will make you take a new look at the old PC, and perhaps extend its useful life for many more years.

Ian Sinclair

Spring 1998

ACKNOWLEDGEMENTS

I would like to thank the friendly and helpful staff of Text 100 Ltd. for providing the MS-DOS and Windows 95 software on which this book has been based, and Word 97 on which it was composed and typeset. I am also grateful to Moira Moles for drawing my attention to the computer recycling firm, RecommIT.

Several of the illustrations in this book are taken from clipart that is packaged with Corel Draw, and I am grateful to Corel Corp. Ltd. for the use of these images.

TRADEMARKS

ABOUT THE AUTHOR

Ian Sinclair was born in 1932 in Tayport, Fife, and graduated from the University of St. Andrews in 1956. In that year, he joined the English Electric Valve Co. in Chelmsford, Essex, to work on the design of specialised cathode-ray tubes, and later on small transmitting valves and TV transmitting tubes.

In 1966, he became an assistant lecturer at Hornchurch Technical College, and in 1967 joined the staff of Braintree College of F.E. as a lecturer. His first book, "Understanding Electronic Components" was published in 1972, and he has been writing ever since, particularly for the novice in Electronics or Computing. The interest in computing arose after seeing a Tandy TRS80 in San Francisco in 1977, and of his 180 published books, about half have been on computing topics, starting with a guide to Microsoft Basic on the TRS80 in 1979.

He left teaching in 1984 to concentrate entirely on writing, and has also gained experience in computer typesetting, particularly for mathematical texts. He has recently visited Seattle to see Microsoft at work, and to remind them that he has been using Microsoft products longer than most Microsoft employees can remember.

OTHER TITLES BY THE SAME AUTHOR

BP 418   Word 95 assistant

BP 421   Windows 95 assistant

BP 422   Essentials of computer security

BP 425   Microsoft Internet Explorer assistant

BP 427   Netscape Internet Navigator assistant

BP 434   PC hardware assistant

BP 437   Word 97 assistant

BP 439   Troubleshooting your PC

BP 446   How to get your PC up and running

BP 447   Multimedia explained

Contents

1 The upgrade option

PC machines have enjoyed a long life, and the feature that distinguishes a PC type of machine from any others is that even the most modern PC machine can still run the software that ran on its predecessor, even back to the first PC that was delivered in October 1981. This 'forward compatibility' has been the feature that has made the PC the machine that has survived when so many others have dropped out or been consigned to supporting roles. You can feel a lot better about updating your computer if you know that you do not have to replace all of your software, because it's the software that makes the computer system valuable.

Compatibility, however, extends only in one direction, and though you can run old software on your new computer, you may not be able to run new software on an old machine. This applies particularly to Windows software, and the use of Windows is a major dividing line between computers we can think of a reasonably modern and those that we have to consider as old. Software that was written for use with the original operating system, MS-DOS, is quite likely to run on a PC of any age, though some modern MS-DOS software may not run correctly on a very old PC.

One option if you have an older machine is to upgrade it. Let's look at the history of the PC briefly to see what is involved, because there have been changes at times that have made upgrading more difficult, and some that have threatened the principle of compatibility.

The story begins with the electronic chips that are used to construct the computer, because when a new chip design emerges the way is clear to redesign or redevelop a computer design. This has happened several times in the long history of the PC, and each major change in chip design marks a change in the features that the PC machine can offer.

The upgrade option

Chips and everything

Small computers are built around the microprocessor chip, a device which was first manufactured in the early 1970s and which has been continuously improved ever since. Intel was the firm that made the first microprocessor chips, and in the later 1970s many small computers used their 8080 chip (illustrated) which dealt with data one byte (of eight bits) at a time. Small computers at that time typically had 4 Kbyte of memory, no disc drives (floppy or hard), and used cassette tape for (rather unreliable) storage. A TV receiver could be used for viewing, though some of the better models used matched monitors. The earliest machines that I used were the Commodore Pet and the Tandy TRS-80, both of which used their own monitors (though some TRS-80s imported into the UK could use a TV receiver as a monitor).

In 1979, Intel developed their 8086 chip, which could work with 16-bit units (2 bytes) and manage up to 1 Mbyte of memory. The 8086 was an immensely difficult chip to make successfully in these days and in consultation with IBM, who took great interest in the development, Intel designed

2

the 8088, a cut-down version of the 8086 which read and wrote data in single bytes (8 bits) but could process it in 16-bit units, with the same capabilities for addressing memory as the 8086. The 8088 had the advantage of being much easier to manufacture and to package, and it could use standard arrangements of memory chips which were designed to work in 8-bit units. Since then, each new design of Intel chip has spawned a new design of PC clones to take advantage of the increased capabilities of the chip.

IBM's interest in Intel arose because of the issue of compatibility. Intel had never developed its microprocessor chips in isolation. Since it first became obvious that the Intel chips could be used to make miniature computers, Intel had marketed each microprocessor chip along with a set of support chips which could be used to manage memory, deal with peripherals such as printers, video monitors and disc drives, and handle control signals (interrupts). In addition, the design of each new Intel chip was a logical development of the previous design, so that anyone who had programmed the old 8080, for example, could very quickly learn to program the 8088; and programs written for the 8080 could be comparatively easily be altered to suit the 8088. This upwards compatibility appealed greatly to IBM because they saw it as a very important selling point in making a late entry into a market in which any form of compatibility was a novelty.

Just about the time that the first IBM small computer, designated as the **PC/XT**, was announced, Intel were developing the chip which would replace the 8088 and 8086 in machines that would be produced (though they might not have foreseen this) for the rest of the 1980s. The 8086 provided the model for the architecture. The 80286, as the new chip was classified, used 16-bit data like the 8086, but the design allowed it to handle the 16-bit units much faster than the 8086. In addition, the 80286 was designed to operate at a much higher clock speed, typically (at the time)

3

The upgrade option

12.5 MHz. At that clock speed, Intel quoted a speed advantage of six times as compared to the 8086 at 5 MHz, and the prospect of making programs run six times faster is one that computer manufacturers and users can never resist. As always, the new chip was constructed so that it could run any code written for the 8088 or 8086, and added only a few codes of its own which have not, because of compatibility problems, been much exploited by programmers.

Speed alone was not the priority, however. Even at that time, when software houses were just starting to take advantage of the memory capacity of the PC/XT machine, Intel were looking forward to the use of machines with much larger capacities, and the 80286 chip was designed to use 24 memory address lines, allowing it to work directly with up to 16 Mbyte of memory. At the time, this seemed too generous.

This amount of memory, however, was not available to existing MS-DOS programs, because MS-DOS is designed to use only 640 Kbyte of memory. Despite this, the AT became the standard office machine to replace the XT. It was well-equipped to do so. Though the machine started life with the old-style keyboard of the XT, this was quickly changed to the 102-key type which was a considerable improvement from the user's point of view, particularly with the provision of indicator lights to show when Caps lock and Number lock were switched on.

The AT also used a small amount of battery-backed memory to hold essential data, and this also maintained a clock circuit so that the time and date were correct when the machine was switched on. This obviated the annoying need to have to enter the time and date into the XT machine each time the machine was used, and this battery-backed memory also allowed other settings, once made, to be retained while the machine was switched off. In addition, the machine was much faster than the XT, and it was this point, coming at a time when many applications programs were becoming larger and slower, that really clinched the acceptance of the machine. Despite this, IBM knew that the machine was really a stopgap which would soon have to be replaced because the AT approach was in many ways a blind alley, incapable of being developed in the direction that IBM wanted to go.

The 80386 chips.

From the time that the AT was launched in 1984, development at Intel was focused on a new chip, the 80386. The aim for this chip was to avoid the limitations that had been built into the 80286, bearing in mind that customers still expected to be able to run PC-DOS/MS-DOS software. At the same time, the new chip should be able to take advantage of a new operating system, or developments of MS-DOS (such as Windows), which could fully exploit its abilities. From the start, the 80386 chip was designed as a 32-bit chip, using 32 bits of data and also 32 bits of address number. This allowed for the use of enormous quantities of memory, 4096 Mbyte, if this could be made available, and it also allowed for the idea of running in different modes to be extended from the simple and inadequate system that had been used in the 80286. This is why the 80286 was often described as a 'brain-damaged 386'.

One answer to the cost of the 80386 was provided by Intel in the form of the 80386SX chip. Internally, the 80386SX is a 32-bit microprocessor, with all the internal facilities and operating modes of the full-blown 80386, but with only 16 external data lines. Quite apart from any other consideration, this means 16 fewer connections to be made, 16 fewer pins on the chip and 16 fewer data lines on the circuit board. Since the introduction of the 80386SX, the full-scale 386 chip was designated as the 80386DX. The price of machines that used the SX version of the chip dropped to an astonishing level, below that of the original Amstrad PC1512, making them a tempting choice for any user.

The upgrade option

The 80486 chips.

The Intel 80486 chip was more of an amalgamation and improvement of chips than a totally new design, and it soon became the accepted standard for the upper end of the PC range. The 80486 is a single chip which includes the equivalent of the 80386DX and a fast memory cache, all on one large chip. The internal design was improved so that the 80486 working at a modest clock rate is much faster than the 80386DX at the same clock rate.

Machines based on the 80486DX were in production for long enough to become established at the top end of the PC market in the first half of the 1990s, and prices inevitably started to come down to about the level that 80386DX machines fetched at the time when the 80486 was introduced.

Pentium and Pentium-2

The 80486 chip had, like the 80386, a comparatively short life before Intel announced the Pentium, a chip that was substantially faster and which is still in use, in various forms, at the time of writing. Early Pentium designs used modest clock rates, typically 75 MHz, but the design has been extended so that the modern versions such as the Pentium MMX and Pentium-2 are using clock rates of 300 MHz and above.

If you have just bought a new computer, it is likely to be a Pentium MMX or Pentium-2 type, so that we can think of any older Pentium types as a previous generation, and any machines using the 80486 or earlier chips, as old computers.

The IBM PC.

The original IBM PC was announced in October 1981, about 16 months after work had started on the design of the machine. The Intel 8088 microprocessor was used along with a set of support chips from Intel, and even by the standards of 1981 the specification of the machine was not particularly impressive. IBM did not initially see the PC as a business machine; even the name 'Personal Computer' indicated that the intended market was the home user, and the price ensured that only the US home user could afford the machine. The standard memory size was only 16 Kbyte, and a cassette drive was used for storage (with a floppy disc drive as an option). What made the machine significant was that it could address memory up to 1 Mbyte and that it used a new operating system called PC-DOS, developed by a small firm called Microsoft.

Comments from customers soon convinced IBM that the home market was much less important than their rapidly-developing business market for desktop machines, and so the machine was re-designed and re-launched as the PC/XT with much more memory (64 Kbyte minimum, expandable up to 640 Kbyte), one or two floppy disc drives and a hard disc option, and optional video boards that could make use of either a colour monitor or a high-resolution monochrome monitor.

This was the form of the PC machine that was to become the standard for business use in the 80s, and which was so extensively cloned. The most important achievements of the XT design when it was first launched in 1983 were that it

The upgrade option

established a standard for 5.25 inch floppy discs with 40 tracks, double-sided, and double-density of recording. This became the IBM standard for the small computers we call PCs.

XT Architecture.

The design of the XT machine was the key to its domination of the business market for computers in the 1980s. Most of the home computers of the 70s and 80s paid little attention to expansion. The Apple-2, however, had a solution in the form of a set of slots in the main chassis (or **motherboard**), into which additional circuit boards could be plugged in order to expand the capabilities of the machine. The IBM XT also exploited the advantages of this 'open architecture' arrangement. No computer has an indefinite life, but if a machine can be expanded to suit growing needs (or has as much as you will ever need in the first place), then the need to replace the whole computer is much less.

Because the machine could be expanded so easily, program suppliers rushed to write software for the XT, confident that the machine would be around long enough to ensure that software would be profitable. In addition, because the use of expansion slots allowed extra memory to be used, programmers could write software that occupied much more than the 56 Kbyte or so that was the usual upper limit of program size for the previous generation of machines. One less favourable point was that standardisation suffered, particularly in respect of video boards. The video board permits the use of a text and graphics display, and the original board supplied by IBM, the Monochrome Display Adapter (MDA) could be replaced by various colour boards like the Colour Graphics Adapter (CGA) and the later Enhanced Graphics Adapter (EGA). This led to the situation that there was no longer a standard IBM PC for software writers, but about seventeen 'standards'. Later PC machines standardised the VGA display that is used to this day.

Even when the XT was launched, the standard form of the machine did not offer outstanding facilities, and it was only by making use of the expansion slots that users could take full advantage of the design. Even such requirements as connection to a parallel printer and a serial modem needed expansion cards, so that the six expansion slots on a standard XT would soon be filled up as owners added what they regarded as essential equipment. There is little doubt that IBM considered the XT as being a machine which would be soon replaced, because at the time when the XT was launched, the development of the AT was well under way.

Another result of the design of the AT machine is that, like the XT, it used parts that were available on the open market. IBM had done this originally so that it could put the machine into production quickly, but it also means that anyone else could buy parts and construct a machine that was, in every way, a PC XT or AT. This is the type of computer we call a 'PC clone', the familiar PC computer of today.

The IBM PC and its clones did not make much impact in the UK, mainly because of high prices, until 1986. In that year, the low-cost Amstrad PC 1512 was launched, and it offered as standard most of the features that buyers of the IBM and of some other clones had to specify as add-on cards. The

The upgrade option

standard memory size, to start with, was 512 Kbyte. This seems fairly insignificant now, but before that time many IBM and clone machines were being sold with 256 Kbyte or less, and the Amstrad machine permitted easy expansion of memory to 640 Kbyte simply by plugging in chips, a ten-minute job. Both parallel printer port and serial modem port were built-in, and the Amstrad was packaged with a mouse for use with the type of software that could make use of it — the mouse and its software alone could cost £100 if it had to be added to other clones. The Amstrad used the 8086 chip, not the 8088, run at a high speed, and was very noticeably faster than the XT machines, while being very closely compatible with the IBM even down to a games program (a flight simulator) which was considered to be the touchstone of compatibility.

The weak point of the original Amstrad PC 1512 was its video graphics. This was not provided on a board slotted in as had been done on the XT machines, but was an integral part of the design, and the CGA type was selected. This permitted the option of a colour monitor, but at a rather low resolution, so that both colour and monochrome displays looked noticeably less sharp than on some (higher-priced)

competitors. The construction and design of the machine, which had the power supply located in the monitor, made it impossible for users to switch to a higher-resolution monitor, meant that there was no escape from the CGA display, and a later Amstrad machine, the PC 1640, used a superior VGA type of graphics board which permitted much sharper displays, particularly colour displays. In addition, the PC 1640 came supplied with the full 640 Kbyte of memory, and made use of the later type of 102-key keyboard as fitted to the AT type of machines.

The arrival of Amstrad stimulated sales of PC clones to an extent that would have been impossible to predict a year earlier and in doing so wiped out many brands of machines which were incompatible with IBM, with each other, and with any sort of serious uses. For a year or more, Amstrad was virtually unchallenged, but by 1988 the pages of computing magazines were filled with advertisements for PC clones of differing degrees of compatibility and specification, many of them undercutting Amstrad considerably. By 1989, many of the original competitors had died out, but the choice of clone machines, XT or AT increased. The AT machine has been the model for later computers that used the more capable Intel chips.

Since the launch of the IBM PC/AT machine, manufacturers of clone machines have been able to capture a very significant portion of the market with machines that feature either very much lower prices than IBM (with its costly dealer and customer support network) could match, or higher-speed specifications. The main target of cloning initially was the XT form of machine, and though many clone machines used the 8088 chip run at the same low clock speed as the original XT, others, notably Olivetti and Amstrad, used the 8086 chip along with a faster clock speed to make machines which were superior in operating speed to the XT.

The upgrade option

When AT clones started to appear, however, the challenge to IBM became more serious. The XT clones could be disregarded as copies of an old machine, a machine which IBM originally saw as a home computer and which became a business standard almost in spite of itself (in some ways because of lack of any effective opposition in this large section of the market). The AT clones, by contrast, aimed at the business market head-on and could not be dismissed as jumped-up home computers. Furthermore, the AT clones which initially made use of the 80286 chip were further developed to make use of the 80386 chip (later, the 80486, followed by the Pentium) and in some cases at prices which so far below those of the current IBM offerings as to be very appealing to the large-scale business user who genuinely required large capacity and fast operating speeds.

Starting at the 80286 end of the market, there was a huge range of clone machines which exploited the advantages of this chip for users whose main aim in life was to run standard MS-DOS applications software faster than was possible using the XT, and with the (admittedly limited) memory expansion that the AT design could offer. The trump card of the 286 clones, however, was the ability to use all of the older XT expansion cards along with later AT-style 16-bit cards, so maintaining compatibility of hardware as well as of software. This type of design became known as ISA, industry-standard architecture, and is the basis of all modern PC machines, though extended now into what is called EISA.

By the end of 1991, however, the 80286 machines were being sold as home computers, and even the 80386SX machines were being aimed at the lower section of the market. The 80386 chip became generally available in 1989, and the SX form of the chip was slow to gain acceptance, though it also became a standard, with every manufacturer offering a model. The 386 successor, the 80486, also became completely established, and by 1991 all major manufacturers

12

were offering 80486 models. It was at this time that the idea of a 'local bus' caught on; meaning a set of connections between the microprocessor chip and the other faster-working pieces of the computer. The earlier type was called VLB, and is used on some 80486 machines, but not on 80386 types. The current type, PCI is found only on Pentium machines.

Can your old PC be upgraded?

Whether or not upgrading is worth while depends heavily on what machine you have for upgrading and what you expect of it. Only comparatively recent machines have large hard drives, large amounts of memory, a fast PCI local bus, and high operating speeds, and some of the really old machines (1987 or earlier) have no hard drive, 5.25 inch floppy drive(s), and only 640 Kbyte of memory. Another important point is that old machines used older display systems such as CGA, and nothing earlier than VGA is really applicable now. There were also machines, mainly from IBM, that used a different form of bus, MCA, that is now obsolete. These machines cannot readily be upgraded.

To start with, we need first of all to have a more convenient way of referring to the various varieties of machines. I shall avoid the need to keep referring to chip numbers and facilities by using the following classification

Name	Chips	Typical facilities
Antique	8088, 8086, 80286	No hard drive, 5.25 inch floppy
Old	80386, 80486	Hard drive, 4+ Mbyte memory, VGA monitor
Modern	Pentium 75 to Pentium 150	Large hard drive, 8+ Mbyte memory, VGA monitor
New	Pentium MMX and Pentium-2	Large hard drive, 16+ Mbyte memory, SVGA monitor

The upgrade option

If your computer is of the *Modern* variety, upgrading is comparatively simple. You can buy an Intel chip replacement that upgrades the chip to MMX standard, though at the time of writing no upgrade to Pentium-2 is being offered (mainly because the Pentium-2 chip uses a different form of mounting). It is possible that chips that offer Pentium-2 facilities but which are a plug-in replacement for the older Pentium will be available from other manufacturers. If the hard drive space is inadequate, it is fairly straightforward to add a second hard drive, and it should be possible to upgrade the memory of a machine in this class to 32 Mbyte or more in line with new machines. This assumes that the existing machine uses a PCI bus and has a modern fast graphics card.

The *Old* class of computer is a much more doubtful proposition because so much more will need to be upgraded. Though chip upgrades are available (at prices that are rather too high to make the action worthwhile), you can be fairly sure that a machine in this class will need much more than a chip upgrade. If it has a local bus at all, it will be of the VLB type, and though this is better than none, it is not compatible with modern add-on boards for the PCI bus. Some machines that used chips from manufacturers other than Intel cannot be upgraded without extensive changes because they used a motherboard that is of a different shape to the standard variety.

80386 machines will have only the earliest type of bus, the ISA type, which is still used on new computers for add-on boards that do not need to run at high speed. Totally upgrading a machine in this class might involve a new motherboard and processor, new graphics board, larger hard drive, more memory, and this could well cost more than a new Pentium computer.

Machines in the *Antique* class are simply not worth upgrading, because literally everything, including the casing,

14

would need to be upgraded. This does not mean that these machines are worthless, as we shall see, simply that it is pointless to bring them up to modern standards. Your options are to use them as they are, to make slight upgrading and use them, or to give them away.

2 The junior option.

As soon as a junior member of your family can read words on the screen, he or she is ready to learn to use a computer. There are, of course, a number of toy computers on the market, and some of them that feature educational software are quite useful for the under 5s, but there are several advantages to be gained from using an older variety of PC machine. For one thing, it's just like yours in appearance, so that it is obviously not a toy, and therefore to be treated with some respect. For another, you can supply the software for a PC, rather than put up with the built-in software of the toy variety, not to mention the noises it makes.

Bytes for kids

Setting aside a spare PC for the exclusive use of the children has a number of other advantages. They learn the use of a full normal keyboard, so that by the time they need to type they already know where the letters are. Some would argue that this inhibits the teaching of touch-typing later, and though this is true to some extent, many learn to type just as fast and as accurately by themselves. In any case, how many children will need to learn the old skill of touch typing now that secretarial jobs are disappearing so quickly? The emergence of voice-to-screen software is also beginning to take a bite out of the need for keyboard use, so that by the time your children are of working age, the keyboard is likely to be an optional extra, used mainly for entering non-standard characters.

Children can also learn to use the mouse. We take the mouse for granted nowadays, but it really was quite an innovation when it first appeared, and children often find it quite difficult to use. They tend to have problems in locating the cursor precisely because they do not realise that the mouse driver software moves the cursor a distance that depends on how **fast** the mouse is moved as well as how **far**. Most children (unlike adults) find graphics tablets much easier to use because the position of the pen on a graphics tables determines the position of the cursor on the screen, there is no speed effect. Learning to position a pointer using the mouse is therefore a skill that has to be learned, and you should not under-estimate how difficult it can be even for older children.

The other argument is that providing a computer for the exclusive use of children is a much better option than that of sharing a computer with adults. Apart from anything else, you may have valuable or private data on your hard drive, an Internet connection that comes into play when you click an icon (with the password stored and used automatically), and a printer which costs a considerable amount to use in terms of paper and ink/toner. Anything that keeps the smaller fingers away from this equipment is desirable.

You can argue that a good password system can prevent misuse, but you will be surprised at how adept children can become at finding passwords or avoiding them. Young learn from old, and at intervals magazines issue instructions for some user who has forgotten a password, and this information trickles down. Good use of a password system can certainly make things very difficult for the unauthorised user, but you have to know how to make your computer secure and how your security measures can be foiled. A locked door (with the key in your pocket) is a much better safeguard than all but the best designed password systems. With a spare computer set aside for their exclusive use, children feel much less pressure to make use of the main computer.

The junior option

Computer age

This is one of the options in which computers of all our categories from *Antique* to *New* can be used. The more recent the model, the greater the variety of software that is available, but you are more likely to want to use software that is not quite the most recent. Apart from anything else, the older software is likely to be cheaper and to have been reviewed in the magazines so that you know what it involves. A large and varied collection of software for an older machine can usually be bought for the price of one new and fashionable item for a new computer.

The age of the computer determines how modern the software can be. If you want to run multimedia CD-ROMs at full speed, you will need a machine of the *Modern* or *New* categories, equipped with a CD-ROM drive and probably also a sound card with loudspeakers. Even a machine in the *Old* class can be equipped with a sound card and CD-ROM, though its speed will not be sufficient for snappy answers. This is not necessarily a handicap if speed is not essential, and children do not necessarily expect instant response unless they have been accustomed to using a machine that provided such facilities.

Antique

A machine in the *Antique* group is not quite so satisfactory as far as software is concerned. The modern multimedia programs are ruled out with a machine that has no CD-ROM drive and no sound system, and these desirable features cannot be added — you can install them physically but the machine can not, and will not, make use of them.

The software will be limited to the MS-DOS variety, and though there are many excellent pieces of MS-DOS software of interest to younger users, there is the handicap of using MS-DOS, which causes more problems for children than the Windows point and click type.

For one thing, typing and spelling are important for running MS-DOS programs, and there is also the important point of knowing which folder (formerly called *directory*) to use and how to open it. If you can write a batch file that allows the user to type a simple word (and press the Return key) for each program, the use of MS-DOS is much less of a handicap, and can be an advantage because it makes the actions easier for the younger users.

This, of course, is possible only if you know to write and set up a batch file, and with the prevalence of Windows this is becoming a bit of a lost art. A good book on MS-DOS will help, and as a guide, here is a set of batch files that I wrote for my grandson. The main file is, in this example, called FRANK.BAT, and it is accompanied by a set of files called PIRATES.BAT, SPELLING.BAT, NUMBERS.BAT and QUIT.BAT. These files are saved in the C:\ folder.

FRANK.BAT contains the commands:

```
cls
@echo off
echo Please select by typing name and pressing
RETURN key
echo
echo    Pirates    Spelling    Numbers    Quit
```

and the other batch files are listed here under their filenames (the filename is **not** part of the file itself).

Pirates.bat

```
cls
C:\games\pirate.exe
Frank
```

Spelling.bat

```
cls
C:\educ\spelling.exe
Frank
```

The junior option

Numbers.bat

```
cls
C:\educ\numbers.exe
Frank
```

Quit.bat

```
cls
Rem Allows return to MSDOS
```

In addition, the last line in the existing AUTOEXEC.BAT file should read:

FRANK.BAT

The batch file will show a menu on the screen when the machine starts up, and this menu will return after a program has been completed so that another choice can be made. Using the *Quit* option will stop the menu action, allowing other programs to be run. The merits of this scheme are that a limited range of programs is on offer, each run by typing its name and pressing the RETURN key. The spelling is not too much of an obstacle, because the names are visible in the menu, and the backspace and delete keys can be used to correct mistakes until the RETURN key is used.

This is only a very simple batch file, and careless use (such as pressing RETURN when the word is mis-spelled) can result in the file ending with the screen showing the C:> message that indicates a return to MS-DOS. You can return to the menu simply by typing the name of the batch file, in this example it is FRANK.

A batch file like this can be enhanced considerably if you know how to write batch files, but it's always better to keep things simple — it does no harm if children find that spelling is important, and that computers cannot make allowance for human mistakes. The merit of such a simple batch file is that it will be easy for you to adapt for other programs, your own programs, and for adding programs to the menu. In the example, you can save the main file with the name of the user, and alter the file references such as C:\educ\spelling to provide the programs that you want to use. The whole system can be expanded to take in as many programs as you want to run, subject only to the space on the screen for the menu.

- Appendix B provides a crash course in batch files if you want to try writing one for yourself.

On this system, then, the user switches the computer on, waits until the menu appears, types a name and then RETURN and uses the software that will then start running. At the end of the program, he/she has to use the program's closing command (pressing some key or key combination), and this will close the program and return to the menu. If a program jams, or an error cause the batch file to stop, no harm is done if the machine is switched off or reset.

Even the oldest machines can be useful running MS-DOS, but if the antique computer is an 80286 model with a hard drive things are much easier. This avoids the problem that children are likely to have with handling floppy discs, particularly the older 5¼ inch type of floppies that can be damaged simply by touching the surfaces with sticky fingers. It is also much easier to ensure that the machine will start up running MS-DOS and your batch file (or whatever you use) because there is no longer the need to ensure that the correct floppy is placed in the drive, and you do not have the same need to worry about backing up floppies.

Old computers

Computers in the old class can range from 80386SX machines to comparatively recent 80486 types, so that what is possible very much depends on where the computer falls in the pecking order. A typical older 80386SX machine with only 1 or 2 Mbyte of memory, a monochrome screen and a single floppy drive of the 3½ inch variety is little better than

The junior option

a machine in the *Antique* class, though it is noticeably faster in action. The video card will probably support the use of a VGA colour monitor (if the machine uses one, or if you can find a suitable one at a low price), and the machine is also likely to have a hard drive. The hard drive on such a machine might be on its last legs if the machine has had a lot of use.

Replacements for old hard drives are not easy to find in shops, but magazines such as *Computer Shopper* are a rich source of older (as well as very new) parts. An important point to remember is that the hard drive type must be the same as the one that is being replaced, though it can be of a larger capacity. Most hard drives in older 80386 machines are of the type described as ST412, but some machines used other varieties, now long-forgotten. Software for such a machine can be of the MS-DOS variety only, but it is usual to find Windows 3.1 installed. Older versions of Windows, such as 2.0 or 3.0 should be discarded.

At the other end of this scale, an 80386 computer might have been taken out of service only recently. Such a machine will typically have a hard drive of 40 Mbyte or more, a memory that is typically 4 Mbyte, a 3½ inch floppy drive, and will run Windows 3.1. With luck, a sound card and a CD-ROM drive will already be present, and if they are not then they can be added. The processor can be the 80386DX or the 80386SX, and the difference, for this purpose, is not important except that the DX machine is more likely to come fitted with the desirable extras.

A machine in this class can run all the MS-DOS software that the lower-level machine can run, and also a huge range of software written for Windows 3.1. If the Windows version is 3.0, you should look for the 3.1 upgrade, because the difference in terms of usability, is very considerable.

Best of all, if the machine has multimedia extensions (CD-ROM and sound), you can use comparatively modern

multimedia CD software, including early editions of
Microsoft Encarta. These will not run at a dazzling speed,
but they do not need to for this purpose, and a great deal of
low-cost CD software is within your grasp. Once again,
magazine articles will guide you to sources of suitable
software. As long as the software was written for Windows
3.1 (rather than for Windows 95) it will be suitable. Some
software that was written for Windows 3.1 runs well on
Windows 95 and the packaging will indicate this. It might
run at a disappointing speed on an 80386 machine, however.
You cannot be certain that software for Windows 95 will run
well under Windows 3.1, however, and it is best avoided.

This is not so important for the educational applications as it
might be for some games, and for a machine in this class you
can buy games for MS-DOS and multimedia software for
Windows. You can also expect to find bargains of software,
because the computer is old enough for wholesalers to be
unloading stocks of older software. In addition, spares for an
80386 are inexpensive, and you do not need to worry so
much if the machine comes in for some rough handling.
Even if you had to replace the whole system you could
expect to pay £100 or less, depending on the level of fittings
and where you bought it.

The best machine in this class is the 80486 type, which is
likely to be well equipped with hardware and will probably
run Windows 95.

Modern machine

The grade of machine that we have labelled as *Modern* is
rather less likely to be turned over to the junior brigade
unless they are older and already well accustomed to using
computers. This type of machine is likely to use Windows
95 (unless you bought an early model from Escom, in which
case you can install Windows 95 for yourself) and it is still

23

The junior option

capable of running all the software that you presently use on a new machine, though possibly at a slower rate.

This implies that the computer will run multimedia software, and this makes it ideal if you want the children to have access to the more recent material such as Encarta 97. The speed, even for the oldest and slowest Pentium models, should be adequate for these purposes, and a further advantage is that if anything goes wrong with the new machine, you can go back to working on the older one until repairs have been made. If you keep a copy of your main software on the machine (preferably with the folders and files protected to prevent accidental erasure or modification) this form of backing up your hardware and software can be very useful.

Other hardware

Printer: Though a computer that is set aside for the use of the children can be by itself useful, the time will come when the users will want a printer, and later on they will really need a printer (probably as they get to secondary school stage).

This does not mean that you have to rush out and buy the latest colour inkjet model, because these are quite expensive to run in terms of ink costs (even for black-only use) and (if you use high quality colour images), paper costs. In addition, there is always the worry that careless use, or attempts to refill cartridges, might spill ink that could be very difficult to clean up.

Laser printers should **not** be considered for this purpose. They should not be used by children except under supervision, because the ozone that they generate needs to be ventilated, and the toner is a very fine powder that cannot be cleaned up with a conventional vacuum cleaner (and I wouldn't like to inhale it either). Though running costs can be surprisingly low, and most of the mechanical parts are under cover, it's better to retain or exchange your old laser printer. Remember that some types, notably the Hewlett-Packard Laserjets can have a very long life because the toner cartridge also includes all the bits that need to be replaced. In that sense, the life is extended each time you replace toner.

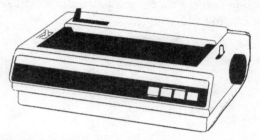

That leaves the good old dot matrix impact printer. Of these, the older Epson types are particularly suitable because they are rugged and long-lived (my old RX-80 has now been in use for some fifteen years), use cheap paper and ribbons, with a further bonus that the ribbons have a very long life and can be re-inked easily and successfully (by an adult) when needed. The only drawback is that such printers can be slow, but not all that much slower than an inkjet. Elderly 9-pin dot-matrix printers are available at low prices if you do not have one to pass on.

- You should avoid the 24-pin type of dot-matrix printer, because these can be more troublesome, with shorter ribbon life and therefore higher operating costs. If, however, you are passing on such a printer that you have used for yourself, that's preferable to buying another printer just for this purpose.

If the children are young, emphasise that printers must not be touched internally — the only permitted actions are putting in blank paper and removing the printed pages. The use of continuous paper is an advantage, provided that an adult changes the paper pile when required. Items such as changing ribbons, altering switch settings, and head cleaning are strictly for adults, remembering to disconnect the printer from the mains supply when any maintenance is being done.

Scanner: A scanner is definitely a luxury item for a computer that will be used by children, but you may just have bought a scanner for the main computer, and so making redundant an old hand scanner.

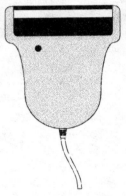

Old hand scanners, such as the well-known Logitech type, are of no value second-hand, and they can be a valuable addition even to a computer system that is used by children because they illustrate that the keyboard is not the only way of acquiring data, particularly graphical data. The older models are likely to work under MS-DOS only, but some later types run under Windows and allow you to see the image appear as you pull the scanner over the paper.

More advanced low-cost types, such as the Logitech PowerPage, use a roller feed to scan a printed page and come with good optical character recognition (OCR) software to convert an image of print into a word-processor file. Very few readers are likely to be passing on hardware of this standard, but if you have always used scanners you may have decided to replace an older type of PowerPage with a colour scanner, perhaps a flat-bed type, so that the old scanner goes the same way as the other older hardware.

When such hardware is available to older children you must take some care over copyright, because the use of a scanner makes it very easy to copy and edit images from any source, newspapers, books or any other paper-based material. This is not a problem if the images do not leave home, but if your children are copying House of Commons headed paper and passing it around the class you could be in trouble. Even enthusiasts for open government usually draw the line at this sort of thing.

3 The word processing option

Working on text

Word processing is one of the main uses of a computer and even a machine in the antique class is likely still to be useful for this purpose. After all, there are still thousands of users who are perfectly happy with pre-PC machines, such as the Amstrad PCW 8256, for all their word-processing needs.

No matter how capable a new machine may be there is always the chance that you need more than one machine for word processing in a household. This, then, provides another use for the older machines. You can turn an old PC around to become a dedicated word processor, along with its printer, used **only** for this purpose. This allows you to set up the computer so that it starts immediately running word processor software, and for some machines this can be much faster than starting up a new machine and loading in the word processor software when you need it.

This use of an older PC is particularly handy if there are two word processor users in the household. Since the old machine has very little real value, there is no reason why it should not be allowed to run all day. This makes its use as a word processor much more attractive, because you can turn to it for writing a short draft, or a longer document, any time you like without waiting for the machine to warm up and load software. If the machine is so old that it has no hard drive then there is practically nothing to wear out, and there is no reason why it should not run all day. The first Amstrad machines in particular had no fan, no hard drive, and were almost silent and have had a very long useful life.

Word processing has been around for as long as there have been PC machines, so that you need not be concerned that there will be difficulties in using older machines and also software. What you cannot do is to use a very modern piece of word processing software, such as Word 97 or the corresponding versions of WordPerfect or AmiPro, on an old machine, even if the old machine can run Windows. If you have been accustomed to using modern word processing software, you may be quite surprised at how very fast some MS-DOS software will run on an older machine.

Use as a dedicated word processor is feasible for a machine of almost any age. Obviously, the later type of machines that can run Windows 95 are able to use more modern software. This, however, does not make them necessarily better word processors than the older machines running older software. Much of the software we use today for word processing is concerned with presentation, rather than simply with printing words on paper.

Presentation is certainly important, but a large part of our writing life is concerned with items such as letters, memos, notes, drafts, and other items that need not be produced as if they were intended for publication and distribution. The acid test is that if your documents could be just as well produced on an electric typewriter, then there is no need for elaborate software, and any age of computer is useful.

One restriction concerning using a really old computer is that it may have to be used with a printer of similar age. It's possible that you have such a printer already attached to the computer, so that there would be no problem about this. You cannot, however, depend on being able to buy a cheap ink-jet printer that will work along with your old computer unless the printer can be configured to accept the codes of an older type, such as the Epson dot-matrix types. Other possibilities are that you might find driver software that will allow a fairly new printer to be operated by old software on an old computer, or that fairly modern software will work on the old machine and drive a modern printer.

The word processing option

Antique

A computer in the antique class will very often make use of a floppy drive only, with no hard drive. This is a considerable restriction in terms of speed of saving and loading software and data, but once the software has been loaded at the start of a session the speed restrictions are much less of a problem. Once again, it is often possible to configure the machine to load in MS-DOS and then to load in the word processing software when it is switched on. This is even simpler if the computer uses twin floppy drives. You might, however, considering replacing the older 5¼ inch floppy drive by the modern three-half inch drive if the design of the computer permits this. At the time of writing, however, 5¼ inch floppies can still be bought new, and any number of recycled floppies can be found at bargain prices.

The printer for such a computer has to be considered carefully. At the time when this computer was new, printers of the laser or ink-jet types were unknown. The most common type of printer in use at that time would be the Epson dot matrix type, and if you have such a printer then it will be ideal. The type to aim for is the RX80 or MX80, because this was a very sturdy and long-lived printer whose ribbon could be used for a very long time before it needed replacement.

The main alternative to the dot-matrix printer at the time would have been the daisy wheel type, and these are still seen in use in offices, and can still be bought, though spare ribbons and daisy-wheels might be more difficult to come by nowadays. As long as a printer uses the standard Centronics type of connection it can be cabled to the PC computer — what you cannot be sure of is whether your software will drive it. You can be fairly certain, however, than an old Epson dot-matrix printer or a daisywheel printer can be used with an old computer.

The word processing option

The restriction on printers is due to the software you are likely to be using. Obviously this will be MS-DOS software, and each piece of software for word processing will contain it own printer drivers. These drivers will be for printers that were current at the time when the software was written. This obviously precludes any printers that have been developed since that time. All such software, however, includes a driver described as *Generic*, that allows no-frills text to be printed. This means the type of text that a typewriter would produce, with no changes of text size or font and other fancy effects.

This may, however, not be such a restriction as you might expect. There are still quite a number of comparatively modern pieces of MS-DOS word processing software available, and if they were written recently, they will contain drivers for more modern printers. You may therefore find that you can use a comparatively modern ink-jet printer along with a computer in the antique class provided that the MS-DOS software that you are using is not as old as the computer.

The main restriction that you will find when using a computer in this class is the absence of a hard drive. For some applications, and wording processing is one of them, you can work reasonably well with floppies, but remember that for the machine of this age the floppy will be the 5¼ inch type and these are not quite so easy to come by now that virtually every machine uses 3½ inch floppies. In addition, the capacity of a 5¼ inch floppy is small, around 360 Kbytes.

One option is to replace the older floppy drive by a new (or second hand) 3½ inch drive. This requires some knowledge of the hardware because some older machines will not accept a 3½ inch drive. Another option is to use an external 3½ inch drive that connects into a parallel port. This is

The word processing option

acceptable if you already have a suitable drive, and if the old PC machine has a second parallel port. You will need the main parallel port for your printer, and port-sharing for this type of use is not on. The snag here is that the ROM of the old computer may not be able to make use of the drive, and this is very much a 'try it and see' action.

By far the best option is the use of a plug-in hard drive if you can find one. These were small hard drives on a plug-in card that fitted into an expansion slot and offered, typically, 20 to 30 Mbytes of storage. Though this might seem ludicrously small by modern standards, it is quite enough to allow a machine such as the Amstrad 1512 or 1640 to operate quickly with suitable MS-DOS software. With such a drive you will find that a machine of the older type, typically new in 1986, will boot up as rapidly as any modern machine, and will run software that is perfectly adequate for routine word processing, as distinct from documents intended for presentation purposes. The problem is to find a hard drive on a card nowadays, and you might have to do some searching through (or advertising in) *Computer Shopper* to find one. If the drive is on its last legs it is not difficult to take the old drive off the card and put in a replacement — if you can find a replacement of the correct type.

To sum up, then, the antique type of computer is in many ways ideal for use as a dedicated word processor. The early Amstrad machines in particular offer the advantage of silent operation, though fans were fitted to later models. Given the use of the hard drive on a card and suitable software, speed should not be a problem, and you can even use a fairly modern printer if the word processing software supports this.

You will still be stuck with the 5¼ inch type of floppy drive, but this also is less of a problem when you do not need to boot from the drive. If the older machine is being used as little more than a glorified typewriter, then transfer of data between this and any other machine is of no importance and all the output will be to paper. If you do need to transfer data to another machine then the options are not so simple. You must either install a modern 3½ inch drive or use a serial link (as detailed in this book) between machines to transfer files. Either way you need some hardware and some software expertise. The book BP434 *PC hardware assistant* is devoted to the type of hardware replacements that you may find helpful.

If your antique computer is of the 80286 type, then it might be much more suitable with less need for upgrading. Even the older 80286 machines came with larger-capacity floppies, typically the 5¼ inch 1.2 Mbyte variety, and some later models used the now-familiar 3½ inch floppy drive. Hard drives are also more likely to be used on the 80286 class of machine.

Old class

The older class of computer typically the 386 or 486 type of machine can cope with a wider range of software. One option is to stay with MS-DOS software, taking advantage of the very high running speed of this type of machine for MS-DOS, and the alternative is to run Windows. A 386 type of machine does not cope well with Windows 95 but can certainly be used with Windows 3.1 or 3.11. The 486 type of machine can run early versions of Windows 95, and if you want to use fairly modern word processing software, you can run Microsoft Word 2 or Word 6 (and corresponding versions of WordPerfect or AmiPro) on such a set-up.

Once again, it all depends on your requirements. If you want simply to produce words on paper you can use fast MS-DOS software and print your documents using the driver that comes with the software. If you want to transfer data, then a machine in this class will almost certainly have a 3½ inch drive, allowing you to save data on floppy to transfer to

The word processing option

another machine. If you run Windows of either variety on the machine, then you have a wider option of word processing software of the more elaborate type available to you. You can run Word 2 under Windows 3.1 or you can run Word 6 under Windows 95. Do not, however, be tempted, even with a 486 machine, to run Word 97 under Windows 95, because it runs very slowly on such a machine and Word 97 does not come into its own until you are using a fast type of computer.

A reasonably modern printer can be used with such machines, because even new inkjet printers come with drivers for Windows 3.1 as well as for Windows 95 and if you are using Windows of either variety you will have no problems in this respect. One of the considerable advantages of using Windows is that you can install a printer driver for Windows, and all of your Windows software will use the same driver. Contrast this with MS-DOS, where each program has to include its own printer driver.

Modern class

The modern type of machine, which will invariably incorporate a chip of the Pentium class, provides an ideal solution to word processing since it allows the use of even quite modern software. For a Pentium machine running Windows 95, Word 97 should be used only if the speed of the processor is high, because Word 97 runs very slowly on machines of less than 150 MHz clock speed.

There will certainly be no problem running word processing software of the class of Word 6, such as the corresponding versions of WordPerfect and AmiPro. There will be no problems in transferring data from these programs to programs running in another computer, but you may find problems if the main computer uses Word 97 and you are transferring data to earlier programs such as Word 6. If you encounter difficulties then try transferring the data in another format, such as Rich Text Format (RTF).

Virtually any modern printer can be used under Windows 95, because if there are no drivers in Windows 95 for the printer you are using there will almost certainly be drivers supplied (either on floppy or on CD-ROM) with the printer. In addition, drivers can be downloaded over the Internet from the Web site maintained by the printer manufacturer.

Commercially available WP software

Microsoft Word. Version 2 is useful and will run under Windows 3.1. Versions 6, 7 and 8 really need Windows 95, and Version 8 needs a fast processor. The earlier versions can be obtained as MS-DOS software for machines that do not use Windows.

Microsoft Write and **WordPad**. These programs are packaged along with Windows. The older of the two, Write, is included with Windows 3.1, and provides sufficient word-processing ability for simple applications. The main snag is that its WRI files cannot be directly by modern versions of Word, but Write can save in the TXT format that any word processor can use. WordPad is supplied with Windows 95 onward, and uses the same form of file as Word.

WordPerfect. This major word processing package has been around for a considerable time, and is available as MS-DOS or Windows versions. The files that it produces can be read by Word.

AmiPro. This was originally called AMI and supplied by Samna, but has been renamed now that it is supplied by Lotus. This is a Windows word processor that was quite capable in its early forms and is a rival to Word and WordPerfect in its present form.

WordStar. This was one of the first great word processor packages for the PC, and it was predominant as an MS-DOS

The word processing option

application in the early years of the PC. It was also, later, produced in Windows form, but has now been overshadowed by the three main applications mentioned above.

WP PD and shareware

A public domain (PD) program is one for which the author has surrendered all copyright, allowing the program to be copied freely by anyone who wants to use it (the way schools used to copy textbooks when photocopying came out of an unlimited budget and books came out of a carefully rationed budget). Many public domain programs are short utilities, and you would normally buy them on a disc that contained 20–50 such items. Other PD programs are distinctly longer, and though some of them do not have the polish of a commercial program they must have represented hundreds of hours of effort. The writers are often professional programmers working at a hobby topic and glad to share the results of their efforts.

Shareware is a rather different concept. The author of a shareware package is hoping to sell directly to the user, cutting out the huge overheads that are involved in having a program manufactured and distributed commercially. In the early days of shareware, the programs were full working versions, and the poor response by way of payment was a severe blow to authors, particularly in the UK, where users were always less willing to pay for programs than in the USA where the idea started. It has become more common now for shareware programs to be limited to some extent, perhaps running on only a single video card, or unable to use a printer or to create disc files. The user can run the program to a sufficient extent to see if it is likely to be useful, and will have lost very little if it is not. Registering with the author can be done directly (it is easy to phone an author in the USA and quote a credit card number) or by way of the PDSL (see below) if this can be arranged. The current catalogue contains many programs of particular interest to DTP users, including clip-art, graphics conversion and editing programs, printer utilities, vector-line drawing programs, etc.

Registration can often be done at various levels, with the minimum level entitling you to a copy of the program with all limitations removed. The documentation will be, as for PD items, as a DOC or READ.ME file on the disc. At a higher fee, a full manual is provided and the user is entitled to upgrades at nominal cost.

The Public Domain and Shareware Library (PDSL) exists to supply discs of programs that are virtually free for inspection, and the only cost to the user is the cost of copying the discs. PDSL can supply on a range of disc formats, and in some cases are virtually the only source of software for some exotic machines. All of the programs are either public domain or shareware. Documentation for each program is included as a disc file, usually with the DOC extension. There are many other suppliers of the same software items, but PDSL was among the first and provides a more full description of the contents of its discs. Like all other reputable PD and Shareware dealers, it also warrants, as far as is possible, that none of its software is pirated commercial software. PDSL is a member of the Association of Shareware Professionals.

The address for PDSL is:

Winscombe House,
Beacon Road,
Crowborough,
E. Sussex, TN6 1UL
Tel: (01892) 663298 Fax: (01892) 667473

Typical word processing programs distributed by the PDSL include the following briefly described MS-DOS programs. Note that some of these, though they run under MS-DOS, feature the use of multiple windows that allow you to work

The word processing option

on more than one document at a time and to copy or move text between open documents..

VDE Ver. 1.7 or higher. Compatible with WordStar files and can read or write WordPerfect and XYWrite files.

Word Fugue is a very capable package that supports a spell-checker and advanced features such as newspaper columns, calculator, word-count, table of contents and index generation and mail-merge. It can be run under MS-DOS from Windows 3.1 and uses its own windows system for displaying and working with more than one document at a time.

PC-Write is a well-established shareware package that includes a spelling checker and the ability to incorporate graphics into documents. Table of contents and index creation are supported. WordPerfect files can be imported.

Breeze is a fairly recent shareware package with the usual features of an advanced word processor plus some unusual additions such as the ability to create self-displaying documents. The software version omits some advanced features such as mail-merge and previewing of graphics printing.

4 The fax option

Fax facts

The conventional fax machine, as used in home or office, is kept permanently switched on so that it can receive a fax message at any time and is always ready to send one. This is not an ideal situation for the small business or home user. The fax machine requires a surprising amount of power even on standby, and some makes will run uncomfortably hot. This may make you feel uneasy about leaving the machine permanently switched on, particularly when it is in your home and you are on holiday.

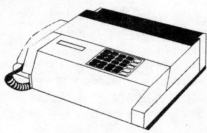

In addition the conventional fax machine uses expensive heat-sensitive paper, and the quality of printing is very poor. There are, of course, plain-paper fax machines, but these are much more expensive despite the use of low-cost inkjet printers. There are also other problems that relate to the use of a conventional fax machine. Any document that is to be faxed must first exist on paper, and that can lead to the ridiculous situation that a word processor is used to create the file, the file is printed, and the paper copy is fed into the fax machine. Similarly in the reverse direction, the fax document will be fed out from the machine and if you want it to be converted to word processor file form, you will have to use a scanner. The problem here is that the poor quality of print from a conventional fax machine makes accurate scanning very difficult.

The fax option

The obvious solution is to use the computer along with fax software and a fax modem. This allows every document to start as a word processor file, and from there to be faxed out without the need to print on paper, unless you particularly need a paper copy. For an incoming fax the image that is received in file form can be displayed on screen, printed on plain paper, or converted to a word processor file by the use of OCR software (optical character recognition) software.

Requirements

Using a computer as the fax machine requires some additional hardware and some software. The main hardware requirement is a fax modem, internal or external, which will convert computer codes into musical notes that can be transmitted over telephone lines, and will also convert the incoming tones from the telephone line into bytes of file data. In addition, you must have a telephone point available so that the modem can be connected to the telephone line which can be shared with your telephones. The modem can be internal, or, as illustrated, external.

The software can be any form of fax software such as WINFAX or Microsoft Fax, to quote two well-known examples. These programs must be run under Windows. Very often, suitable software will be bundled along with a fax modem so that if you need to buy a modem you should ensure that suitable software is provided. If you already have a modem then you probably also have fax software.

The modem along with the software provides for sending and receiving faxes, assuming that all documents, text and graphics, originate as word processor or graphics files. This accounts for a large percentage of all the documents you are likely to deal with, but there may be occasions when you need to transmit the contents of a paper document. If this is likely to arise frequently you will need a scanner, and there are many scanners of good performance available at low prices. Look, for example, at the Black Widow range, whose Web site is at http://www.blackwidow.co.uk/scanners. You may wish to have the scanner connected to the main computer rather than to a computer that is used as a fax machine, and transfer the file by way of a floppy.

Using an older computer as a dedicated fax machine allows it to be left permanently switched on and connected to the telephone line. The software can be configured so that the incoming ringing tone will start the fax software or you can use an external hardware fax switch that will route the incoming call to the computer or to a telephone answering machine as required. In addition, using an older machine for this purpose avoids the problems that could arise if your main computer might be packed to overflowing with junk fax messages, as can happen. What we now need to consider is how suitable machines of different ages and specifications would be for this use.

Antique class

The antique class of computer has certain advantages that you might think made them suitable for fax use. Machines that have no fan will run silently and this makes their use an advantage if they are to be left switched on permanently. On the other hand, antique machines may have no hard drive either, and a hard drive is very important for fax use since the software and the data will occupy a fair amount of disc space. In addition, an antique machine will not be able to run Windows, so that you will need to look for software that can run under MS-DOS, and such software is not exactly commonplace (though not unknown or impossible).

The fax option

Since it is most unlikely that a computer in this class will already be fitted with a fax modem (though it might possibly be fitted with an old slow modem, unsuitable for fax), we really have to rule this class of machine out for fax uses. There is just too much to do both in terms of hardware and software to make machine suitable. An exception might be made for some of the better 80286 machines because these used modest hard drives and some of them could run Windows 3.1, allowing for the use of more modern fax software.

Old machines

Machines in the older 80386 and 80486 category are much better suited for use as dedicated fax machines. They will quite certainly use a hard drive of reasonable size, and will almost certainly be equipped with Windows so that they can run the more modern fax software. If noise is a consideration, these machines can often be used with the fan speed reduced so that they can be left running permanently without too much disturbance.

If the machine has not been used for fax purposes before, then the addition of hardware and software will be needed. The hardware, of course, is the fax modem, and the software will generally come bundled with the modem. All that remains is to ensure that a telephone connection is available reasonably close to the computer. You might also want to install a hardware fax switch that can direct fax messages to the computer and telephone messages to the answer-phone or to the telephone.

Some preparation will be needed. The hard drive should be cleared of everything that is not really necessary. The essential software is, of course, the operating system (MS-DOS and Windows) along with the fax software. You will need some word processing software and some software that will deal with graphics. If you are connecting a scanner then you will need suitable scanning software as well. You may, however, want to run the scanner with the main computer and transfer the results by floppy drive or by a serial link between the computers. If you are concerned with messages as distinct from presentations you can use comparatively simple software that does not require a lot of disc space. For example, you can use Write or WordPad for documents and Paint for graphics, all of which are included with Windows.

This should leave a reasonable amount of space on the hard drive for fax data, both in and out. Remember that the data coming in will initially be in the form of a graphics file and such files take a large amount of space. Typically, a machine in this class will have a hard drive of around 100 Mbyte which should leave ample space for fax, word processing, and graphics software if you avoid the larger packages. The memory of a machine in this class is likely to be 4 Mbyte and if less is present it can easily be upgraded. Suitable memory now costs much less than it did when the computer was new.

Modern machines

Machines in this class have the considerable advantage of ample hard drive space and equally ample memory. They will also be equipped with Windows 95, and may even already have a fax modem built in so that no hardware effort is needed to make such a machine suitable for use as a dedicated fax machine. The only handicap is a high noise level, because such machines use a processor fan in addition to the fan fitted in the casing. Though the main fan can be made to run slower and so with less noise, you would have to be quite certain that this was acceptable from the point of view of adequate cooling.

The main changes that would have to be made concern the contents of the hard drive, stripping out everything that is not needed. This would leave: the operating system along

The fax option

with fax software, word processing software, and graphics software. You can exchange files with the main computer by using floppy discs, or by using a serial link between the machines. As before, a scanner might be fitted to the main machine, or you might feel that it would be useful to connect the scanner permanently to this second machine to relieve the load on the main machine. Since many new machines come with a rather small number of ISA slots, it is an advantage if extra ISA cards are fitted to the second machine rather than to the first.

Details

Whichever age of a machine is concerned, you can see from the above that some hardware will need to be installed, and almost certainly some software also. If you are totally unfamiliar with any sort of hardware installation work then you might like to take a look at BP 434, the *PC hardware assistant*.

Most of the hardware changes that are needed for fax involve little more than fitting a card into a slot. This is straightforward, and the main point to watch is that an internal fax modem is a thick card, often taking up the width of two slots. This can make fitting difficult if several of the slots are already occupied. Fitting an external fax modem is much easier because the machine need not be disturbed. Some users prefer the use of an external modem because its operation can be monitored (by observing panel lights) and it can be switched off if you want to avoid incoming messages. The external modem is connected by way of a serial link, with no need for an extra slot. The snag here is both serial ports might already be in use. For example, you might have a mouse connected to one serial port and a link to the main computer connected to the other one. For machines that use the PS/2 type of mouse port, there should be no problem in finding the spare serial socket.

If more hardware effort is needed, you might question whether the machine is really suitable. The *Old* class of machine in particular may need more work than is reasonable, and if you are unaccustomed to hardware fitting you might balk at the thought of such an effort.

5 The Internet option.

Internet requirements

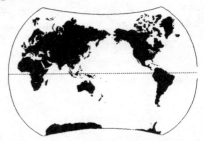

The requirements of a computer for Internet use hinge as much on the modem as on the computer itself. This means that a fairly old computer can be used successfully for browsing the Internet provided that the browser software will run on that computer. For older machines this rules out the use of the most recent software, such as Microsoft Internet Explorer, and since the Internet in its present form has not been around for as long as the PC machine, there is not much software around that can be used on really old machines. To use the Internet, then, requires software that runs under Windows.

- Another point to note is that the additional software that is needed to make connection is usually supplied by the Information Provider (IP) on CD-ROM, so your computer needs a CD drive to read the software. Some providers will offer the alternative of floppy discs.

The hardware that must have priority for any computer used for Internet access is a faster modem. At the time of writing the fastest modems available are the 56K type, but some older computers might not be able to cope with this modem speed using an external modem because of an old type of serial port incapable or running at such a speed. Even the earlier 34K type of modem, which is satisfactory for many

46

purposes, may be faster than some older serial port hardware can cope with.

Remember that when the spare computer is being used for Internet access, speed is not quite so important as it is when you are using your main computer, and tying it up so that nothing else can be used. When an internal modem is used, it will contain its own fast serial port, so that the port that is fitted to the computer is irrelevant. You will also have to subscribe to an Internet supplier (an information provider, IP) and you will be charged for your telephone use, usually at the local-call rate.

By the time that you turn over a discarded computer to Internet use, you may have the option to connect other than by a modem. At the time of writing, the only alternative was the ISDN type of connection which needs a different interface (though the term *modem* is still used, and these devices cost more than the telephone-line type of modem). ISDN (meaning integrated services digital network) is currently very expensive in start-up and running costs, and lower-cost systems are being developed. Of these, the most promising is the scheme to link to the Internet by way of the electricity supply system. This seems likely to provide very low cost Internet access so that long periods of connection would not be expensive, and an entirely different interface would be required. The attraction here is the possibility of a fixed annual charge for unlimited access, with no large telephone bills to worry about. Another possibility that is already a reality in some areas is Internet connection by way of a cable TV company.

- Whether these types of connection would run on an older Windows machine or not cannot be determined at the moment. Once again it is likely that handicap of an older machine would be the limited speed of its serial port.

The Internet option

Since you would normally specify a fast modem for Internet access, you could very easily combine this with fax facilities. In fact, it would be unusual nowadays to have any fast modem that was not suitable for fax use, so that you could very easily hive off two functions that require modem use to the spare computer instead of cluttering the main machine. This also has the advantage of freeing up some ISA slots on the main machine, remembering that an internal modem usually covers the width of two slots. As far as equipping the machine is concerned, Internet and fax can use the same modem, but different software. Provided that the computer has adequate hard drive space for the software, there is no problem about combining these actions.

Antique machines

The antique type of machine is not necessarily handicapped for contacts with bulletin boards, but Internet access use requires more modern Windows software. The speed of Internet access depends much more on modem than on computer speed, and the crucial factor in this is the speed of the serial port rather than that of the computer. The problems relating to using an antique machine are to be found in its lack of a hard drive and in its inability to use modern software.

Much depends on your requirements. If you need true Internet access then you simply cannot use an antique computer. Even though, in theory, such a machine might be able to cope with Email requirements, the software that is currently available is almost entirely designed to be run under Windows. For an antique machine that is equipped with a hard drive, adding a modem is simple and will allow access to useful facilities such as bulletin boards, but Internet browsing is definitely ruled out.

The difference is that a bulletin board can be contacted using any communications software (a terminal program, such as the Hyperterminal of Windows 95). You can find suitable software for even the older computers, because some varieties run under MS-DOS and do not need Windows of any variety. The Internet allows to make world-wide contacts by dialling one number, and the software has to include data-processing ability to cope with connections to a large variety of computers.

Old computers

The types of computers that fall into the old class are rather more suitable for Internet access use than the antique types. These machines will almost certainly be fitted with a hard drive, and so they can cope with more modern software, Windows in particular. The 80486 type of machine in particular is likely to have enough hard drive space, to have a reasonably fast serial port, and to process quickly enough even for Windows software. Windows in this sense means the earlier Windows such as 3.1 or 3.11.

A later 80486 machine will probably be using Windows 95 and can run the less demanding, older, versions of Internet browsers — *Netscape Navigator 2* is a useful choice for such a machine. If all that you want from the Internet is to browse text, participate in news discussions, and use Email, then you can obtain low-cost software that will be perfectly adequate for these purposes, running under Windows 3.1 or Windows 95, and can run as fast as is needed. If, however, you need to work with graphics, or to make use of features such as security systems and censorship systems that are included in modern Internet software, then the older type of machine is ruled out

The machines in this class may already be fitted with a modem, though this might be, by modern standards, a fairly elderly and slow modem. Now that the prices of fast modems have fallen to a reasonable level, you might feel

The Internet option

that the machine deserves this enhancement to make it suitable both for fast Internet access and for fax use.

Remember that an internal modem is likely to cost significantly less than the external type, so that this type of modem is more desirable — it does not need a separate mains supply, for example. It is likely that there will be an ample amount of spare ISA slots on such a machine, so that it would be pointless to consider any other type of modem, particularly since an internal modem incorporates its own fast serial port. Machines in this class should be adaptable to the other means of Internet access discussed earlier.

Modern class

The modern class of computer is likely to be faster, contain a larger size of hard drive, use more memory, and run Windows 95. It may also already have a modem fitted so that it is ready for Internet use right away, needing only connection to the telephone line.

This is ideal if you need to run modern software such as Microsoft Internet Explorer in any version above 3.0. If you need to buy a modem for this machine then you should use the fastest modem that you can find since this class of machine can do justice to it.

One point to watch is that this type of machine may provide more spare slots for its local PCI bus than will be available for ISA cards. Remember that an internal modem will require the width of two ISA slots, leaving little room for other cards of that type. For a second computer used in this type of dedicated way, however, this is not of great importance since few other cards are likely to be needed. The greater facility in terms of hard drive space and in memory size make it possible to use a machine in this class for more than simply Internet access and you can consider using such a machine for all the tasks that you might want to remove from the main machine.

Typical IP installation

Assuming that the computer contains a fast modem, runs Windows, and has reasonable resources of memory and hard drive space, you have to install software from an information provider (IP) in order to have Internet access. This is a decision that ought not to be rushed.

There has been a price war on Internet provision, so that a large range of prices will be on offer. Most providers offer a local telephone number for access, which is in itself a considerable saving — ignore any provider that cannot offer this through, for example, a 0345 or 0845 number. You can obtain some further relief from the dreaded bill if you notify BT that your IP contact number is one of your frequently-used numbers.

Another point to consider is the scale of IP charges. Many IPs publicise a £4.95 low-use rate, and if you use mainly Email with very little net browsing (or none) then this may be perfectly adequate. Some IPs offer extended services, but these are not necessarily useful to you and they provide another layer on top of the main browser software (nowadays almost always Microsoft Internet Explorer or Netscape Navigator). This extra layer can slow down the action and often provides services that you do not particularly want. If you intend to use the Net fairly extensively for browsing as well as for Email you should consider a fixed-cost contract, usually of around £100 per year. One firm with such all-in contracts is Global Net.

Another point to watch is that several providers are of US origin, and some of them appear, judging by the time taken, to check your status and password using a computer in the USA. This all adds time to your telephone call, and makes actions like checking how much you are being charged both lengthy and expensive. A local provider can be much faster and less expensive, but this is not necessarily true as you

The Internet option

will find if you shop around. In some cases, shopping around can be difficult because you do not find out the scale of charges unless you install the software and give your credit card details.

Most IPs will supply connection software on CD-ROM, so that if your computer does not use a CD-ROM drive you will have to see if the software can be supplied on floppy discs. The CD-ROM discs are often attached to magazines or can be sent to you by post on application. If you use Windows 95 or Windows 98 you need only insert the CD-ROM into the drive to run the software and start the IP installation, which will also install a browser (Microsoft Internet Explorer 4 at the time of writing) and Email and News software (usually Microsoft Outlook Express).

Whether or not the IP offers a month's free trial, you will be asked for your credit card number. There is no way round this, and you will not be connected unless you quote a valid number, which can also be for a debit card (like Switch or Connect). If you opt for an annual fixed fee for unlimited access, make sure that you pay by direct debit and that you do not start paying until your free month is up.

The setup of the link should be fairly smooth, but there may be some hiccups. One common one is that the IP provides you with a password that you cannot remember. This is usual if you have to facility to use an Email name with extensions for the rest of the family. In such a case, you will want the password to be entered automatically when you make contact, avoiding the need to type in the password each time. If you find that the option to enter the password automatically is greyed out and cannot be ticked, you will have to follow the advice in the Help pages for the browser. This usually involves altering the connection details to state that you are connected to a network, and that the name of the network is Microsoft.

Make sure also that you know how to change the password. Some providers allow you a password of almost any length, others confine you to six letters only in the main password. Remember that any password that is easy to remember is probably easy for anyone else to guess.

IP software provides for the password to be stored in your computer and used automatically. If you use your computer exclusively this can be convenient, but if your computer is shared, particularly by younger members of the family, you might want to opt not to store the password in the computer. Once again, you should find out how this action is carried out.

6 The test-bed option

Why use a test-bed?

The idea of using a spare computer as a test bed may seem rather exotic but it is very useful if you frequently need to make use of new software, such as the software that comes from CDs attached to magazines, or to try out software, particularly software that has been downloaded over the Internet.

Software from unknown sources, and particularly software that has been downloaded from anything other than a trusted manufacturer's Web site, has to be treated with some degree of suspicion. Software in CD-ROM form, in particular the large amount of software that is bundled with magazines, is less likely to cause problems, but it may include beta software that can crash a system, or software that you want to try out before adding to the main computer. This is particularly important if the software would take a large chunk out of your available hard drive space on the main computer.

The main hazard of software that has been downloaded from the Internet is that it can spread a **virus** to your system. Rather a lot is made of this, particularly from those software writers who want to sell anti-virus software, but the hazard

does exist and if you are in the habit of downloading software from sources you know nothing about then you ought to take some precautions at least.

The worst scenario is that a virus will be downloaded with such software and will cause extensive changes to your hard drive which in the worst case might require total reformatting of the hard drive. If you keep some form of total backup, such as a tape or read-write CD drive, that will backup your entire system, then even this virus effect might not stop you working, but it would certainly represent a setback that you could not afford. If you do not keep and regularly update such a backup then you must either use anti-virus protection or try out new software on a different machine whose contents you are less worried about.

The extensive amounts of software that come with magazines (usually the same set of titles on all the magazines!) have been carefully tested for virus contents but the problem is very often that you are uncertain if the software is useful to you, and you certainly would not want to clear out your hard drive simply to make space to try out some new long program. In addition there is always the problem that some programs will leave remnants behind even after an uninstall system has been used.

There are now several pieces of uninstall software that will clear out the remnants of a deleted program from your hard drive. These, however, are not infallible, and it is better by far not to install software unless you know that you really want it. The use of a spare machine is much better in this respect than installing new software into the main machine, finding that you do not really want to keep it, and then trying to get rid of it.

There is, then, a good case to be made for using a second machine that would otherwise be scrapped for carrying out this type of testing. This is a less costly option than using elaborate anti-virus software, and avoids the problems as

The test-bed option

described of installing and uninstalling programs. It also allows you to test really extensively programs that you might be reluctant to test on the main machine, such as re-partitioning and re-organising the hard drive or other utilities which, if they happened to cause problems, would cause very serious problems on the main machine.

A machine used only as a test-bed need not be connected to a printer or other peripherals, so that there is much less to do in the way of hardware enhancements than for other applications covered in this book. The main snag is that the spare machine has to be capable of running the software that you want to test.

Backing up

Software for backing up the hard drive has been available for some time, and a backup system was included in Windows 3.1, but it was, by general consent, not regarded as particularly trustworthy. The backup system provided with Windows 95 (and in Windows 98) was, by contrast, excellent. Backing up is a precaution against losing files due to a hard-drive failure, and it also can ensure that you have a copy of files that existed before a virus infection.

You should certainly use backup on your main computer, and if you are intending to use a spare computer for testing programs you should consider some form of backup, even if only to floppies, for this machine also. In the event of the Windows system being corrupted, you can then re-install from the backups or from the original CD-ROM. Remember that if you re-install from CD-ROM you will not re-install the exact system that you had before the crash, because few users of Windows use it in its default state. It is more likely that you spent several hours configuring Windows to run the way you wanted it (you may even have altered the registry) and it is rather a daunting task even to try to remember what you did.

Backup is one of the *System Tools* set of Windows 95. It allows you to backup data in compressed form on floppies, tapes, other computers on a network, or removable hard drives. You can also use it to compare a backup file with the original, and, obviously, to retrieve files from the backed-up form. The process is automatic once it has been started, though if you use floppies you may need to change discs at intervals – about 4 Mbyte can be saved on each floppy. Only a few types of tape drive (such as the Colorado Jumbo) are recognised by Windows 95 *Backup*, and if you use other types you will need to use the software that comes with the backup system. Windows 98 provides for other systems, including the use of 120 Mbyte floppies.

To start a backup under Windows 95, click the *Start* button, followed in turn by *Programs*, *Accessories* and *System Tools* From the *System Tools* set, click *Backup*. You may want to create a shortcut to this for future use. The main *Microsoft Backup* panel will appear. You will then see a list of folders and files in Explorer format, with a small box next to each name. Click this box to place a tick into it and so select it. Selecting a drive will select all folders and files on that drive. Selecting a folder name will select for backup all the files in that folder. You can also select file names individually. If a large number of files is selected the process can take several minutes.

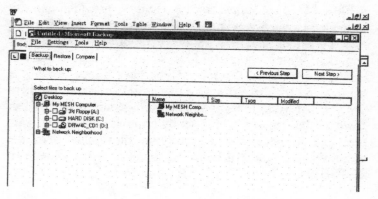

The test-bed option

When files have been selected, you can click the *Next Step* button. This selects a destination for the backup, and the two most likely are **floppy drive** or (if you have a tape backup) **tape**. Make sure that a blank floppy or tape is inserted into the drive, and then click the *Start Backup* button. You will be asked to type a filename for your backup, and a useful type of filename is the date (such as 8JUN98) along with an indication of the contents (DATA, SYSTEM, PROGS, etc.). When you have done this the backup will start. If you are using floppies you will be prompted to change discs at intervals.

- You should label these floppies in sequence, as they will need to be inserted in the same order when you restore the contents.

If you are likely to back up the same selection several times, you can save it as a *file set*. This is particularly useful if you have selected several folders, because if the contents of the folders change, they will still be automatically selected for backup because the folder has been selected. The file set can be saved after you have selected a destination for the backup by clicking File — Save As in the menu, and providing a filename for the selection. This is saved as a file of type SET and can be obtained subsequently by using File — Open File Set the next time you make a backup.

A file set for *Full System Backup* (FSB) is provided and can be loaded in when you are asked to select files. An FSB will back up all of the files on the hard drive, including the important Windows registry files, so that you should make at least one backup of this type if you have a tape drive or a removable hard drive (the size of the FSB makes it unlikely that you will want to use floppies for this purpose). You can decrease the size of the FSB set by removing from it all data files and, if necessary, all program files other than the Windows set. You will be asked to confirm any change to the FSB set.

The Settings — Options menu allows you to specify options for general use and for the three main actions of Backup, Restore and Compare. The *General* options boxes provide for turning on audible prompts and for overwriting old status log files. Both of these can normally be ticked, unless there is some particular reason for retaining old log files.

The main *Backup* option box is labelled *Quit Backup after operation is finished*, and this can be ticked if you want to resume normal working as soon as possible after making a backup. You can also choose between making a full backup on all selected files and making an incremental backup only of files that have changed since the last full backup. See later for details of incremental backup.

The *Advanced* section has four option boxes. The *Verify backup* data box will automatically carry out a file comparison between the backup copy and the original and report on any differences. The box labelled *Use Data Compression* should be ticked, particularly if you are backing up to floppies, as it makes full use of the available storage space. The option to *Format if necessary on tape backup* provides for using unformatted tape. The option of *Always erase on tape backup* allows the same tape to be used over and over again for a full backup, and must not be used if you want to make incremental backups on the same tape. The last option is *Always erase on floppy disc backup*, and this also is usually desirable unless you want to avoid the possibility of wiping a disc by mistake.

The main option of the *Restore* section is the *Quit Restore after operation is finished*, and you will probably want to tick this option. You can also choose whether to restore backup files to the *Original location* (the default), to an *alternative location*, or to an *alternative location, into a single folder (directory)*. The use of an alternative location allows you, for example, to place all of your files on a new hard drive (added in parallel with the original), and the use of a single folder allows a set of files, originally from different folders, to be restored to a single folder from a backup so that you can find them all without having to search through a set of folders. One point to watch here is that the filenames must not be duplicated.

The *Advanced* section provides for verifying restored data against the backup copy, and the options for files of the same name are *Never overwrite files, Overwrite older files only*, or *Overwrite files*. If you use this last option you can opt for a prompt message each time a file is to be overwritten.

In the *Compare* options the *Quit after operation is finished* option is available. The file comparison options are *Original location, Alternate location*, and *Alternate location, single folder (directory)*.

The other options provide for *Drag and Drop* and for *File Filtering*. The Drag and Drop options allow you to specify how you want Backup to proceed when you have the Backup program displayed as an icon and you have selected files and dragged them to the Backup icon. The options are to *Run Backup Minimized*, to *Confirm Operation before Beginning*, and to *Quit after Backup is Completed*. File filtering allows you to specify file types (in the form of extension letters) that you want to exclude from a backup, or to exclude files on the basis of date.

You can opt for full or incremental backup of the files you have selected. A *Full backup*, as the name suggests, backs up the files completely, so that they can be restored to the state they were in at the time of the backup. An *Incremental backup* can be made only following a full backup of the same files, and it backs up only the changes in files. This action should be reserved for specialised purposes, because it does not back up new files that have been added to folders, only changes in files that were previously backed up. You must clear the *Always Erase on Tape Backup* option box before you add an incremental backup to a tape that contains an existing full backup. When you recover files, both the full backup **and** the incremental backup files must be present.

The Backup software is essentially the same as is provided for the Colorado Jumbo tape backup system (a Hewlett-Packard product), but the Colorado software also allows for restoring the contents of a hard drive after a catastrophic failure which has required replacement of the drive. This uses a System (Startup) floppy disc with the Colorado software on it. There is no provision for this action in the Microsoft Backup version, but if you use the Colorado drive, you can prepare floppies for this type of emergency, but use Microsoft Backup for your normal backup actions.

- The types of tape drive supported in Windows 95 are of the built-in QIC 40, 80 and 3010 type, manufactured by Colorado, Conner, Iomega or Wangtek; or the externally connected parallel-port QIC types manufactured by Colorado. Other drives are not recognised, and must use their own software – this applies to the popular Travan type of drive, and any drives (such as CD-ROM writers) connected by way of a SCSI interface.

- The log files for backup are called Error.log and are located in the Program Files — Accessories — Log folder, normally on the C:\ drive.

At the time of writing, the Colorado Jumbo tape drives are obsolescent, and you may be able to find tape drives of this type at an attractively low price. Tapes are comparatively expensive, but the price reflects the amount of data that can be saved. The cost of tape storage is lower than that of high-capacity floppy discs, though more than read-write CD media.

The test-bed option

Virus testing

Hard drive viruses are a menace which affect very few hard-disc users, but which, like terrorism, cause more worries and expense than real damage. A virus is, strictly speaking, a piece of code which can attach itself to a program and reproduce itself so that it can be transmitted to other programs and also from one computer to another. The term is also used of other unwanted codes which can be loaded into a computer and which from then on will cause problems to appear, whether these can be spread to further computers or not. The virus is activated and spread when the program that it has contaminated is run — if you don't run the program you don't activate the virus, and if you don't copy the program you don't distribute the virus.

The main types of virus are the Boot Sector type which locates itself in the boot sector of the hard disc and loads in whenever the computer is booted, and the Parasitic virus, which is attached to a program file and is activated when that program is run.

The problem is not one that affects machines that run only floppy discs, because a floppy disc with a virus can be thrown away. You can hardly throw away your hard disc if it is infected. Viruses are not effective on data files, because data files are not composed of instructions, so that the virus instruction cannot be executed. No virus has ever been found in the CMOS RAM memory of any PC computer.

A virus can affect your computer only if you load and run a program from a disc that contains the virus, or if you load software over the telephone lines by way of a modem and then run it. Millions of computer users who do not use a modem and are careful about where they buy software are at no risk of virus infection. Many viruses are comparatively harmless, like graffiti and have been devised by programmers wishing to demonstrate their skills.

The Trojan Horse is not really a virus, but it can cause just as serious problems. It takes the form of a program with an interesting title. When the program is loaded and run, it carries out the damage.

The Worm is also not really a virus but it reproduces itself within the computer that it affects until so many copies have been made that there is no further room on the hard disc. It also has a serious effect on networks.

Bombs, also not necessarily viruses, come in two forms, time bombs and logic bombs. A bomb program, once loaded, saves itself on the disc and does nothing until some condition is met. A time-bomb will be activated by date (like Friday 13th) or time (like midnight) and will carry out its action if the computer is running at this time. A logic bomb will operate when other some conditions, such as 65% or more of the disc being used, or a copy of some well-known program being installed

The true virus will attach itself to programs, and if these programs are copied to other computers this will allow the virus to be spread.

What do they do?

A virus may simply put up a message of the 'Kilroy was here' variety on your screen, but at the other end of the scale it may cause files to vanish from your hard disc directory. This damage is not necessarily irreversible, but even if it is not it can take a long time to sort out. The really destructive viruses are fortunately rare.

Always be suspicious about unsolicited gifts of discs such as demonstration discs. If in doubt, try them on an old floppy-only machine. Discs that have been run in a large number of machines are also suspect, as they could have picked up a virus from an infected machine. Programs from unknown sources on the Internet are also a prime source of viruses.

The test-bed option

The earliest types of virus programs were comparatively simple. They usually altered the COMMAND.COM file, and could be counteracted by checking the size of this file regularly and re-installing if necessary. Later types of viruses are much more ingenious, using a variety of techniques to conceal their presence and to evade virus-detecting software.

The sequence of bytes used by viruses can often be used to detect a virus, and some now use code that is varied each time the virus reproduces. A few portions, however, need to be kept in sequence and can be detected. No Anti-virus program is nearly as effective as taking care not to become infected

Windows 3.1 contained the MWAV program which could be used as a way of checking for and deterring the entry of a virus. These utilities were omitted with Windows-95 because they were incompatible, and if you want virus protection software for Windows 95 you will have to buy one of the third-party type from such sources as McAfee or Norton.

Let's put the problem into perspective. I place several hundred floppies and CDs into my computer each year, and have never had a virus. No-one else uses my computer, I do not use the modem to download software, and I get all my discs from the manufacturers. If your system is used like mine, you are not in danger. The best method of dealing with viruses, computer or biological, is not to become infected. As far as your computer is concerned, you might not be in any danger.

Viruses reach your hard-drive program files either from a floppy disc that you have used to install something, or from a program that you have received by way of the modem and run. Files that contain only data will not pass a virus, and programs that you run from a floppy and which do not install anything on the hard drive are also innocent. You can, however, find that a word processor document contains a macro program that can install a virus, and if you use Microsoft Word you will find advice and software to deal with this problem.

Beware of gifts of discs. Obtain programs only from reputable suppliers, whether these are commercial programs or shareware. Never run games programs that are passed on from another user. Try out suspect discs on a floppy-only machine if you can.

Beware of demonstration discs or system checking discs that have been inserted into a large number of computers. Keep adequate backups of all program files on floppy discs. If all else fails, you can reinstall a 'clean' program from these discs.

Machine age

A machine that is used for test purposes must be able to make use of the type of programs that you want to test. These are almost certain to be fairly new Windows 95 programs, so that the spare machine must be capable of running such programs. This points to a machine in the *Modern* or *New* category.

In addition, such a machine needs to be well equipped. If you want to test software that comes on CD-ROM, then the machine must be fitted with a CD-ROM drive. This need not be the most up-to-date fast type of drive, and you may already have a suitable drive on the machine. If a drive has to be added, the older 4- and 6-speed CD-ROM drives are now very inexpensive.

If you are testing programs that are downloaded from the Internet, it is more desirable to download directly into the test-bed machine than into the main machine, since this removes any chance of virus contamination in the main machine. This calls for a modem in the test-bed machine unless you can be quite certain that you can avoid running a

The test-bed option

downloaded program. This is easy if you use an external modem, because you need only change the serial cable from one machine to the other. Another option is to link the computers by a simple network and download (using the modem in the main computer) to the hard drive in the spare computer.

7 The programming option

Programming

Programming means writing the instructions that will make a computer perform some task, small or great. The computer hardware itself is useless without a program, just as a CD player is useless without the little discs that carry the information and cost so much. Once a computer is running a program, it obeys the instructions of that program, and no others. The program may allow the machine to seek some response from you, in the form of pressing a key, typing a word, moving the mouse or even making a sound, but the machine's reaction is pre-planned, built into the program and it will accept only what it is programmed to accept.

Now the reasonable question to ask at this point is why should you program the computer for yourself when for a few thousand pounds you could have as many professionally-written programs as you might need? The figure of a few thousand pounds is one good reason in itself if you are a home user or you use the computer in a small business, though for the average Mega-Euro corporation this might be chicken-feed. The one single overwhelming answer to this question is that only by programming for yourself do you get exactly what **you** want.

Remember that when you buy a program written by someone else, the program is in charge and it decides how you have to proceed. When you write your own program, you are in charge, and you decide what the program produces. If you don't need VAT paperwork, the program doesn't produce it. If you want printed receipts, your program provides them. If you need a list of customers in alphabetical order, your program can be made to give that, or a list in order of how much they owe you, it's all up to you to decide what you want and arrange for it to be supplied. Control is the main reason for wanting to program, whether you use your computer for business or for pleasure. Some of this can be provided by using an applications package with a macro language but the macro language itself is a form of programming.

There's another reason, which has nothing to do with business but a lot to do with curiosity. You can use a computer as you might use a car, putting up with its odd little ways, but never doing anything to understand them. Using a computer in this way is never entirely satisfying — you always feel that the machine will have the last word. Just as by understanding what makes a car tick (or run smoothly as the case may be) you can drive it better and avoid breakdowns, you can also, by learning more about the computer become able to make better use of it. Computers are still at a comparatively early stage of development. It would not be an exaggeration to say that small computers are today in much the same state as cars were when the Mini was introduced. In any case, the more you know about the machine, the better you can drive it.

In addition, programming is a very considerable aid to thinking. When you learn to program, you also learn to break a problem down into manageable pieces, and work on the pieces. If you are programming for some business reason, you'll learn a lot more about your business from writing the program, than you imagined possible. If you program for a hobby reason, then both your hobby and your computing will come on in leaps and bounds. Programming is the most stimulating mental activity that there is, and you don't have to start at Professor level to get a lot from it — just watch a class of 8-year olds at work with a computer.

Programming languages

A program for a computer is a set of instructions, and a programming language is concerned with how these instructions are written. When you **use** a computer, as distinct from programming it, you use commands. When you use MS-DOS you type each command and press the RETURN key. When you use Windows you do not need to type these commands, only to point at the command icons and click or double-click the mouse button. In a program, the words of command are written in the sequence in which we want them to be carried out, but they are not carried out until the program is run. The words or codes that are used to define instructions in a program are what make up the programming language, along with the way that the words must be used, which is the **syntax** of the language.

At the bottom of the heap of programming level comes machine code, writing directly in number-codes. Machine code consists of a set of numbers, with each number making up one tiny part of a command. Machine-code programming is tedious, error-prone and very difficult to check. Each new chip has its own machine-code (the microprocessor chip is the machine of the title) and one advantage of working with the Intel chips of the PC machines is that their machine codes are either identical or very similar.

The only good reasons for using machine code are that it's the only way to program a completely new machine for which nothing is written, because of its speed, and because of the control that it gives you. There are always features of a machine that can be controlled only by machine code, and if you want to have your screen scrolling diagonally, or to run an unusual disc system, or to use a non-standard printer you might need machine code to write the routines.

There is such a continuing need for machine code that we need a programming language, called **assembler** (or **assembly**) language, in order to write machine code with less tedium and fewer bugs. Assembler language comes slightly higher up the scale compared to machine code, because it's easier to write, but it still produces fast machine code. If you want to write short and comparatively simple

The programming option

routines that will execute rapidly, like routines to set up a printer, then assembler language is a very useful way to produce such material. It's quite another matter to produce a large program in assembler, however. Here's an example of assembler language which allows your typing to appear on the screen when running MS-DOS:

```
mov ah,08
int 21
mov dl,al
mov ah,02
int 21
cmp al,1a
jnz 0100
int 3
```

An assembler program would convert this set of commands into a set of code numbers, and save these codes as a program that you could run under MS-DOS.

At the other end of the scale a **high-level language** looks, when you read a program, almost like a set of instructions in English. This is called the **source-code** of the program. When you write programs in a language of this type, you don't expect to have to worry about the details of the machine. You aren't interested in what microprocessor it uses. You don't need to know about ASCII number codes, or where routines are stored in the ROM, or where to store data in the RAM, or any of the things that constantly occupy the minds of assembly language programmers. You simply write your program lines, run them into the machine, and sit back like anyone else until the program crashes.

The language processor (an **interpreter** or a **compiler**) converts the instructions of your source-code program into machine code, and the computer then executes the machine code. The name 'high-level' is a good one — you are so far above the ground level of machine code that you hardly know there's a machine there. Needless to say, the language is the same no matter which machine you happen to be programming.

Between the high-level languages and the ground level of machine code and assembly language, there are languages at all sorts of intermediate levels. The fundamental problem is that high level languages are powerful but inefficient. They allow you to turn your problem-solving methods into programs that run smoothly, but at a great cost in memory space. They can be cumbersome, using lines and lines of program which can take all day to compile, and which might not run very fast afterwards.

At the other end, machine code is very compact, very fast, very efficient — but sheer hell to write and debug (remove errors) in any quantity. The reason that we have such a large number of programming languages is that we are constantly trying to get a better balance of these different virtues. What most programmers want is a high level language that makes it easy to express the solutions to problems, is reasonably compact both in statement length and use of memory, and which translates into almost as few bytes of machine code as would be given by an assembler.

There's no such language, and probably never will be, but some come nearer than others, and some are a better solution for some kinds of problems. Nowadays there is also a demand for languages which are fail-safe, used for purposes such as defence software and systems for aircraft control. The over-riding requirement for such languages is the avoidance of errors, something that is exceptionally difficult in large programs. Another modern requirement is for languages that make use of Windows, and these are distinguished from the MS-DOS variety by adding the word 'visual' to the title.

One good way of starting programming for the ordinary user is the language that is called Basic. The letters of BASIC mean Beginners All-purpose Symbolic Instruction Code, and

The programming option

that's what it originally was — a simple language that was intended to serve as an introduction to programming, and modelled on one of the great original computer languages, FORTRAN.

The advantage of the original Basic was that it was very simple to learn, but close enough to the methods of FORTRAN to make the conversion easy. Basic could be provided in interpreter form (see later), so that mistakes could be easily and quickly found and corrected. Finally, a Basic interpreter could be written in code that took up only a small amount of memory. It was for precisely these reasons that when microcomputers became available, they featured Basic as their programming language. There was no off-the-shelf software in these early days — you wrote your own programs to carry out what you wanted to do.

The Basic program could be put into the same ROM as held the operating system, so that from the instant that the computer was switched on it had a programming language ready to use. The original PC machine had a Basic called BASICA in ROM form, and this Basic has greatly influenced the types of Basic that are available on the later PC machines.

Here's a sample of a fairly modern Basic:

```
CLS
a% = 10
INPUT "type a number, please, between 1 and 20
       (ENTER)"; b%
IF a% > b% THEN
  PRINT " My number was larger than yours"
  PRINT " I shall reduce it to zero"
  b% = 0
  PRINT " My a% is"; a%; " and your b% is now"; b%
  END IF
END
```

The programming option

Since the early days of using Basic as a way to FORTRAN, Basic has developed a long way. As the language grew, it acquired more features from other languages, and without losing its simplicity, soon became a major language in its own right, not just a path to an almost-forgotten FORTRAN. Because of the intensive use of Basic versions on small computers, the language has become a general-purpose one, good for all kinds of programs whether your interests were in accounts, science, engineering, text editing, or whatever. Other languages tended to remain specialised, good for only one or two selected purposes (sometimes only for teaching purposes), while Basic grew to fit the needs of users.

Nowadays, more people can program in Basic than in any other language, and they don't necessarily learn it so that they can learn another programming language, such as C. After all, you don't learn English so that you can later learn Icelandic or Sanskrit. One particular advantage of Basic, however, is that it has inherited all the mathematical actions of FORTRAN, so that if you want to program for engineering or scientific purposes, Basic is still an excellent choice and is widely used. The Windows version, Visual Basic is widely used to write utility programs for Windows.

Compilers and Interpreters

Most computing languages can be obtained in either a compiled or an interpreted form. Whatever language you use to express your program ideas, it has to be converted into machine code before it can be used in the computer, because the computer can work only with machine code. Interpreting and compiling are two different methods of carrying out this conversion, and if you have used only BASICA on the PC, or some variety of Basic on another machine, you will probably be familiar only with interpreting.

Interpretation requires a program, the **interpreter**, to be running in the memory of the PC and working on each instruction of your program. You cannot run a program that you have written unless you first start the interpreter running. Compiling, by contrast, uses a program, the **compiler**, to convert each instruction of your program into code that will from then on run on its own (as a COM or EXE program file). Both interpreters and compilers have merits and faults.

The main merit of an interpreter is easy correction of errors, known as **de-bugging** (a bug is an error in a program, a de-bugger is a program for correcting errors, and the cause of the errors is called a programmer). When your interpreted program stops with an error message you can change the program text and try again. For a compiled program, correction of an error would mean loading in the text of the program (the source-code instructions written in the form of English suited to the language), compiling it, linking it with existing routines and then running again, which is inevitably a slower process. The disadvantage of the interpreter is low running speed, because the process of finding the machine code routines can be a lengthy one, and it has to be done each time an instruction is obeyed. The ease of use of the interpreter is paid for by slow running, and the high speed of the compiler is at the expense of easy checking and changing.

- The ideal system is to develop the program using an interpreter and then to compile it. This is possible using some varieties of Basic that allow the same source-code to be used either for an interpreter or a compiler.

Principles of programming

Before a program can be written for a computer to use, the action of the program must be planned so that it can be carried out by a sequence of steps. For very simple tasks, like making the computer operate a printer direct from the keyboard so that it acts like an electric typewriter, this can be done in one step with very little effort by one person. For large-scale tasks, like automating the stores system of a warehouse or controlling a production line, the planning must be on a much larger scale, with several people each allocated a section of the work and one person responsible for the overall plan.

By dividing the work into sections, then breaking down these sections into smaller and more manageable pieces, each piece can be made small enough for a single programmer or a small team to work on. The most difficult part of such a programming task is to ensure that all the pieces of the program fit together afterwards, and this can be made much easier by choosing a suitable programming language which is designed to be used in this way. Nowadays this is often achieved by using a language version which is described as being *object oriented*.

The actual **coding** of the program, writing down the instructions for the computer, is the least important part of the act of programming. Many newcomers to computing place a lot of emphasis on learning a programming language, and worry about whether their chosen language is the most suitable for their future uses. This is a mistake, because learning to break down problems into small pieces is the most fundamental part of programming, and the chosen language is much less important, though the correct choice of language can make the final conversion of plan into program much easier.

It is most likely that anyone who starts programming now will have to learn more than one programming language later, simply because languages tend to be suited to specific purposes and are constantly being revised. A language that is well suited for writing programs for office routine work may be unsuited for working on engineering calculations; a language that is admirable for learning the principles of programming may be quite useless for writing fast-moving

The programming option

graphics routines for animated displays that demonstrate the working principles of a new invention.

Programming fundamentals

No matter what programming language is used, the task has to be broken down into pieces that are small enough to work on without confusion, and these pieces are called **modules**. Some programming languages demand that the pieces are very small, others are less fussy, but the types of pieces are much the same for all languages, and it is these types that we have to look at now. The computer may have to deal with numbers, with letters and words, measured quantities, sound or graphics; all of which will be represented within the computer by number codes. Programming languages, apart from assembly language, are not concerned with the details of the codes, but they do work with the quantities that are converted into these codes.

All programming languages allow you to use a limited number of instruction words (also called reserved words), the words that must be used for instructions. For an extended Basic like BASICA this number can be large, 120 or more. It's still very small, however, compared with the thousands of words that a *natural language*, like English, uses, and one of the problems of learning programming is trying to express what you want to do with such a limited number of instruction words.

This means that you have to break down any problem into small pieces that can be tackled by using a few of these reserved words of the computing language. Basic deals with this by having a large number of these reserved words, but other languages use a small number of reserved words and allow you to pick ready-made routines from a library held on a disc to make up other actions.

Each reserved word or keyword has to be used in a very precise way, the syntax of the word. If you don't use the word correctly, the instruction cannot be carried out, and you will get an error message that reads *syntax error* to draw your attention to it. Programming means precision and how you use and place words is important in a programming language.

Programming teaches you to analyse problems, and to tackle them with precision and that can't be bad training for anything in the business world. If you can program for your business needs, then it is likely that you understand your business better than those who cannot program. Programming is an analytical skill akin to formal logic, and when you learn to apply this skill to business needs, you will learn much more than you ever thought possible about these business topics.

Using the spare computer

If you are interested in programming, it makes a lot of sense to learn on a spare computer. For one thing, most of the programs you will be practising with will be short and will use MS-DOS rather than Windows, so that you might not want to have to switch your main computer to MS-DOS in order to work with these programs. Another point is that it's easy to lock up a computer with incorrectly written instructions, and you have much less to lose if you lock up a spare computer. If you work with assembly language you can carry out actions directly on the disc system and a mistake can scramble a hard drive. You would not want to do that with your main computer.

The main thing when you are beginning to take an interest in programming is to choose what language to use. For the newcomer the choice should be Basic, and if you want to learn quickly, you should use an interpreted Basic that runs under MS-DOS. At one time, a version called GW BASIC was included with MS-DOS, and an older PC might have GW BASIC on its hard drive or on a floppy. The next step

The programming option

up from this is QBASIC, supplied with later MS-DOS versions. This is interpreted, and is less easy for a beginner, though ideal if you have some experience and want to write something useful. A later version called QuickBasic was compiled and is an excellent way of creating programs to run under MS-DOS. In addition, the source-code of QBASIC can be compiled using QuickBasic. At the other end of the Basic scale, Visual Basic is designed for programming in Windows, and it is so unlike the older types of Basic (or anything else) that it forms a topic of its own.

Now let's see what different grades of machines have to offer for anyone starting to learn programming. For making this start, the use of an interpreted Basic like GW BASIC is ideal, and it can be used on any PC computer, old or new, as long as the computer will run MS-DOS.

Antique class

A machine in the *Antique* class is as good as any for this purpose, because you will be working with short programs that require next to nothing in terms of disc space, so that the absence of a hard drive is no great handicap, nor is a monochrome screen display. If you intend to do any assembly language programming, a simple machine is greatly preferable because there is less to go wrong if a program misbehaves.

In addition, a machine in this class will start up in MS-DOS rather than in Windows, and you can arrange to start the machine running your Basic interpreter (if this is put on the same floppy disc as the operating system). A twin floppy drive or a hard drive is a bonus, but even if you have the most primitive PC possible you can still use it for learning Basic, either interpreted or compiled. Remember that the compatibility of the PC means that if you write a compiled Basic program on your old machine it can be run under MS-DOS even on a new computer.

Old computers

The computers in the 80386 and 80486 class can be run using either Windows or MS-DOS, and if you want to use them for learning programming using an interpreter or compiler running under MS-DOS you will find it an advantage to disable or remove Windows. Windows 3.1 can be disabled by removing from the AUTOEXEC.BAT file the last line that consists of the instruction word WIN, and Windows 95 can be uninstalled from a computer — you will be able to re-install it if you need it by using the original distribution disc (CD) or discs (floppies).

This leaves you with a machine that can run a Basic interpreter or compiler very fast and efficiently, because the hard drive allows a fast start, and you can arrange the AUTOEXEC.BAT file so that the interpreter or compiler starts immediately after loading MS-DOS.

This class of computer can also be used with Visual Basic which runs under Windows and creates Windows programs. Visual Basic was originally advertised as a system that was easy to learn, but it requires a pretty good knowledge of programming to get anywhere with it. If you have had any experience of programming in the past (not necessarily with any variety of Basic) you can try out Visual Basic for yourself on any machine that runs Windows. The earlier versions of Visual Basic, particularly version 2, are easier if you are new to this system, and you should be able to get hold of a copy at negligible cost. Modern versions are very expensive, but there are alternative systems advertised on the Internet.

Modern class

A Pentium computer can be run under MS-DOS just as easily as under Windows, and you can use the F8 key when you start the machine to ensure that you start in MS-DOS. Another option is to start the machine using the Startup disc

The programming option

in the floppy drive so that only MS-DOS is loaded. You can also, of course, allow the normal start into Windows 95 and then switch to MS-DOS. The other option, as for the *Old* class of machine, is to uninstall Windows 95.

All that has been said regarding the older type of computer then applies, and you have the usual choice of interpreter or compiler for Basic, or to use Windows 95 and learn Visual Basic.

Programs for programming

There is no shortage of programs for writing in Basic or in other languages, but this does not mean that they are easy to find. Older versions on MS-DOS came with the GW Basic interpreter, and because an interpreted program will stop when an error occurs and provide you with an error message, this is an ideal way to learn. Later versions of MS-DOS came with the QBASIC interpreter, which offers a better variety of Basic. There is also QuickBasic, which is a compiler and though this is less easy for the learner it does allow you to write programs than can be run on any PC (it does not need the compiler to be present when the program runs).

Visual Basic was not normally packaged with Windows or with MS-DOS, so you will almost certainly have to buy a copy. The Visual Basic system uses a compromise between interpreting and compiling, so that a machine will run a Visual Basic program only if certain files (such as VBRUN200.DLL) are present.

The trouble is that nowadays it can be quite difficult to find sources of older Basic interpreters or compilers. Oddly enough, this is because so many copies were given away with MS-DOS. Suppliers see little point in stocking a program that was given away for so long a period, and if you find a supplier advertising programming packages (rare enough now) you will find that they cater for the professional programmer rather than the newcomer, and at prices to match. You can, for example, be asked to hand over more than £1,000 for the latest professional version of Visual Basic.

Your best approach is to look at small adverts, particularly for older versions of MS-DOS on the original discs, if you want to find GW-BASIC or QBASIC. For the few who are attracted by assembly language, the best assembler is an old program called A86 which at one time was available as shareware, but is hard to find nowadays. You may be able to find the old versions of Basic on the Internet if you look around, and A86 may still be available from some shareware sources. Using the Internet Search facilities will turn up a lot of references, but does not help in finding the program to download, so that you have to know where to look and how to phrase a question. Using the *Yahoo* or *InfoSeek* search engines you will find a large number of references to the search request 'Basic Interpreter', and several of these offer downloads of interpreters old and new. There is, for example, a new interpreter (Yabasic) available free on the site:

http://www.uni-mainz.de/~ihm/basic.html

and *Infoseek* will come up with a large number of the older interpreters on the site:

http://www.intermid.com/basic/download/htm

and also on

http://www.civeng.carleton.ca/csce/software2/p0007.html

There are another 185 pages of references for this search request, including some varieties that operate under Windows, so that you are fairly certain to get something useful. If you have acquired some knowledge of working with Basic, it can be interesting to try out some of the new interpreters and compilers from these sites.

The programming option

There are many other programming languages, but some are intended for specialised purposes, and others need a firm grasp of programming principles before you can make much use of them. The merit of Basic is that it is the nearest we have to an all-purpose language, and it can, initially at least, be comparatively simple to learn.

Books

If you are starting programming you will certainly need at least one book. A lot of books on programming are directed to academic needs, and are not easy to follow if you are starting from scratch, so you will need to look for books that were written for the beginner who is interested in the subject rather than intending to make a career of it.

Most of these books are now out of print, because the rise of Windows has been accompanied by a drop in the numbers of readers interested in programming. A book called *Starting MS-DOS Assembler* from Sigma Press deals with the A86 assembler program, and was in print until fairly recently. Books on GW Basic are not easy to find now, but one published by Glentop might be in your library. Two of my books, *QBASIC Beginners Book* and *Visual Basic Beginners Book* were published by BSB and though these are no longer in print you can sometimes find a copy in a shop, and certainly in libraries. BABANI (who publish this book) have a very wide range of inexpensive books including BP284 *Programming in QuickBASIC* and BP346 *Programming in Visual BASIC for Windows*. A stamped addressed envelope sent to BABANI (address on first page of this book) will ensure you receive a complete list of titles.

The Internet can also be a good hunting place for books, and you may be able to locate copies of books that are out of print in this way.

8 Odds and ends

Other uses

There are, of course, many other uses for a computer that is no longer the newest on the block, but we shall confine ourselves to computing uses rather than to applications like doorstops or footrests. As it happens, there are several applications that can make constructive use of a discarded machine and which do not fall under any of the headings that we have considered so far.

Teletext receiver

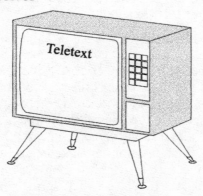

Teletext has been a feature of TV receivers for some considerable time, starting around 1978 in a few up-market models such as the Pye CT480 (which was also one of the first receivers with remote control). Over the years, modern receivers have incorporated this useful data service as a standard item, which is totally free to any TV owner. One enhancement that has never appeared on mass-produced TV receivers, however, is the ability to print the teletext pages. Printing is a very valuable enhancement, because several teletext items run to more than one screen page and because it is very tedious trying to write out the content of a page while viewing it on the screen. Despite this TV receivers never appear with any type of printer port, or even a serial link to allow the text to be transferred to a PC.

There is, however, one way of printing teletext pages that is available to any owner of a PC. This is to install a teletext card inside a PC computer, connect it to a TV aerial, and so download the text information which can, of course, be displayed on the screen and also printed by the printer that is connected to the computer. Using the computer for teletext in this way avoids the need to switch between pictures and text on the TV receiver, and allows storing of the pages in addition to displaying and printing. These stored pages are in image form and can be converted, using OCR software, into word processor files if required.

The snags are threefold. One is that a TV aerial may not be within easy reach. The other is that the main computer may not have space for yet another ISA card. The lack of an aerial point is the more serious, because set-top aerials are without exception useless for teletext reception except when you are really close to the transmitter. If you have a roof-top aerial that provides a strong signal, you can split this using a specialised distribution amplifier and continue to feed one or more TV receivers while also providing a signal to the card in your computer. In an area of strong signal another possibility is to place a second TV aerial in the loft space and run a separate cable to the computer.

The solution to the ISA slot space is, as you will know by now, to use a spare slot in an equally spare computer. This also gets round the usual problem of having the main computer tied up while you are viewing teletext pages. The main item to consider is the software that comes with the teletext card. If this can be run under Windows 3.1 then the spare computer need not be of the most recent type. It is, however, unlikely that the antique class of computer would be useful, because it runs only MS-DOS and it lacks a hard drive and may even lack a VGA type of screen.

The third snag is cost and availability. You will have to search for any advertisements for a suitable card, and the cost will be around £70—£90. There are several cards that are used to take TV signals live or from video recorders and which deliver a selected still picture to graphics software. Many of these do not deal with teletext, because teletext is used in the UK only. The TV/video cards made by ATI and Hauppage, however, offer teletext capture as well as picture signals. The Hauppage card is a PCI type, the ATI card is ISA fitting.

Any machine in the *Old* or *Modern* class, however, should be able to cope with an ISA card and the software so that it can be used as a specialised teletext receiver. This also avoids tying up the main TV receiver, and it allows more time for browsing the full set of teletext pages on all terrestrial channels.

Note that though you will find a *Teletext Channel* on the Internet (using Microsoft Internet Explorer) this does not provide the page structure of the TV version, so that you cannot look up, for example, a recipe that appeared on a teletext numbered page. If you want to use teletext as a form of newspaper that you can print out, the Teletext channel can be useful, though the search facility may come up with an error message (script file failure).

Networking to a modern computer

There is yet another type of assorted use for the retired computer. This applies particularly to a machine with a reasonable amount of hard drive space. The scheme is to connect the spare computer to the main computer in a simple network. You can arrange things so that you have access to all the drives of the spare computer from the main machine, and you can, if you want, have access to the drives of the main computer from the spare computer. Though the spare computer can be kept in another room, it is easier to use this system if both machines are close to each other, because both must be switched on to make use of the file-sharing actions.

This can be a very useful way of backing up files from the main computer, storing files that are not immediately required, and of providing facilities that you need only occasionally on the main computer. Remember that the spare computer need only be switched on when it is needed, and with its intermittent use the hard drive will have a long life.

- Note that this also allows a printer to be shared, or for one machine to use either its own local printer or a printer that is connected to the other machine.

Obviously, anything like this requires both hardware and software, and the software is already incorporated into the later versions of MS-DOS (and a different form is built into Windows 95, including the OSR2 version installed in new computers from 1997 onwards). The hardware consists only of a cable connecting the two computers. If you are content with a leisurely rate of data transfer, or for transfer over a distance of more than a metre or so, you can use a serial cable.

For much faster transfer you can use a parallel cable, but this introduces a few complications. One is that the parallel cable is **not** the same as is used for a printer, but is differently connected, and with the same type of D-shaped plug at each end — a printer cable has a 25-pin D-plug at one end and a Centronics flat-connection plug at the other. The other point is that this system ties up the parallel port in each computer. If the spare computer is not connected to a printer, then this is of little consequence since there will be a parallel port free. On the main computer, however, which will be connected to a printer, a second parallel port is desirable. This will take up one ISA slot, and though the parallel port card is simple to fit you have to configure it as LPT2 or whatever else (LPT3 or LPT4) you want to use other than LPT1.

- The older Interlink software will be found in the MS-DOS or DOS folder and it consists of two files called INTERLNK.EXE and INTERSVR.EXE. On the most recent computers with the later version of Windows 95, or supplied with Windows 98, there is no DOS or MSDOS folder, and the INTERLNK files are not present in the C:\WINDOWS\COMMAND folder that contains the other MS-DOS commands. On an older machine with MS-DOS 6.0 to 6.22 you should be able to find these utilities.

Interlink is intended as a simple utility for connecting a laptop to a desktop computer, but it can be used as an elementary form of network system for two computers, using either parallel or serial ports. Most computers possess only one parallel port which is used for the printer, but it is quite common to fit two serial ports and even if one of these is used for a serial mouse this leaves one spare for the Interlink connection.

- Interlink does not rank as a network, and if a program asks you during SETUP if you are running on a network, answer **NO** if you use only Interlink.

Since the use of serial links is much more common, this will be described in more detail. Serial links, using a modern serial port, allow transfer rates of just over 115,000 bits per second, which is considerably slower than can be achieved with parallel ports, but fast enough for printing or file copying. The hardware consists simply of a seven-core serial cable of the type called **non-modem** or **null modem** terminated in the type of plugs that the machines use — either a 25-pin or a 9-pin type.

- Serial cables that are intended for connecting printers or external modems are useless — their connections

87

are not suitable. You should specify that you want a non-modem (or null-modem) connected cable for linking two computers together. If a parallel cable is used it must be of the bi-directional machine-to-machine type. These are unusual, and though you can buy cables described as bi-directional (for use with inkjet printers particularly) these are not suitable because they have a Centronics plug at one end.

With Interlink in use two machines can share disc drives and printers. One machine is designated as the **server** and the other as the **client**. The client can be used normally, with the drives and printer of the server at its disposal. During this time the server is immobilised — you cannot use it normally. You would therefore make your main computer the client and the spare machine the server.

Interlink can be used in a variety of configurations, and you need to decide for yourself, after trying some out, what will be best suited for your own uses. Interlink, though it runs under MS-DOS, can be used along with Windows on either machine, though task switching cannot be used while the machine is being used as a server.

The minimum requirement to use Interlink is to add the command INTERLNK.EXE in a CONFIG.SYS line to the machine you will use as a client, your main computer. You might want to use this line in the CONFIG.SYS files of both machines to allow yourself some flexibility. A typical CONFIG.SYS entry is:

    device=c:\msdos\interlnk.exe

which will install Interlink (whose files are, in this example, in the *msdos* directory) and look for a connection as the computer is starting up. This connection need not exist at that time and can be started at any time later by using INTERLNK or INTERSVR, see later.

The options that can be used following the INTERLNK.EXE command are:

• **/DRIVES:n** Interlink assumes three drives. If you have fewer or more on the other computer you can specify them as /DRIVES:2 or /DRIVES:4 for example. If you use /DRIVES:0 no drives will be shared, only printer connections.

• **/NOPRINTER** Ensures that the printer is not shared. Remember that if a printer is shared both machines must be switched on and running Interlink before printing can be done from the machine that does not have the printer connected.

• **/COM** Can be used in the form /COM:1 to specify a serial port (usually in the range of COM:1 to COM:4) rather than have Interlink find it for itself.

• **/LPT** Can be used in the form /LPT:2 to specify a parallel port, LPT2 in this example, for data transfer (NOT for the printer).

• **/AUTO** Creates a link only if the server is active, otherwise does not load Interlink into memory.

• **/NOSCAN** Installs Interlink in memory, but does not attempt to link with the server.

• **/LOW** Installs Interlink into conventional memory rather than the (default) upper memory.

• **/BAUD** Used to specify a serial transfer rate if for some reason (like an old and slow serial port) the normal rate of 115,200 cannot be used. The slower rates are 57,600, 38,400, 19,200 and 9,600 and they will make access noticeably slower.

• **/V** Prevents timer conflicts - use this if, for example, a serial mouse stops working when Interlink is running.

Odds and ends

When the INTERLNK.EXE line runs in the CONFIG.SYS file it establishes a set of new drive letters, equal to the number of drives on the other computer that can be shared. If the number of drives on the other machine is not the default 3, you should use the /DRIVES option to correct this. It is also useful to add the /NOSCAN option if you often start one machine alone or at a different time from the other.

• If you do not share a printer then add the /NOPRINTER option because this reduces the memory requirements of Interlink.

• The /COM option can also be useful, particularly if you use a serial mouse on the COM1 port. Using /COM:2 in INTERLNK.EXE prevents the program from checking COM1 and possibly interfering with the mouse action.

The normal use of Interlink involves starting the INTERSVR program on the server machine (your older computer) and INTERLNK on the client (your main computer.

On the server machine, run INTERSVR, either direct from DOS or by way of Windows. This will show only the outline window when the other machine is not yet activated. On the client machine, start INTERLNK either at the MS-DOS command line or by clicking on the command in DOSSHELL or Windows.

• If you are running Windows you can click on a drive letter that is linked to the other machine instead of running INTERLNK.

The screen of the **client** machine will then show a list of equivalent drive letters and the display on the server machine will change to reflect the connection. The connection remains in use until it is broken by pressing Alt-F4 at the **server**. The server diagram remains on screen as a reminder of the connections. For example, the C:\ drive of the server machine might be referred to as F: on the client machine, so that a command such as:

COPY F:\words*.TXT C:\text

can be used. For most purposes it is easier to use Windows 3.1 File Manager or Windows 95 Explorer to carry out such actions.

Running INTERLNK from Windows 3.1 in the client machine presents no problems, but when INTERSVR is run the INTERSVR menu remains on screen. You cannot make use of Windows actions like task switching on the server machine while INTERSVR is running A message will appear to remind you of this.

You may have problems in some cases with different MS-DOS versions. Normally, provided that one machine is using MS-DOS 6.0, the other can be using any version from 3.0 onwards. This is not true if the server machine uses a single large disc partition, as is normal, and the client is using MS-DOS 3.0 to 3.4, because these versions cannot make use of large disc partitions. You may also have difficulties if your main (client) machine is running a later version of Windows 95 or any version of Windows 98.

If you use the Client machine to run a program that is located on the disc of the Server you need to be sure that the program is one that could run on the Client (not configured for a different video system, for example).

You should not attempt to use hard drive tools over an Interlink connection. The safest way of using this type of connection is to hold only data files in the old (server) computer and to load or save these files from the current (client) machine. This allows the server to be used as a form of backup for data.

Odds and ends

If your older computer is in the *Modern* class and runs Windows 95, it is likely that the MS-DOS Intersvr and Interlnk files will not be present. The alternative is to use the system called *Direct Cable Connection* that is provided in Windows 95 and Windows 98. This software can be used with either a serial or a parallel cable — as before, the parallel cable has to be suitable for this purpose, and the Help list of Windows 95 shows a US supplier only. If you do not find Direct Cable Connection in your Start — Programs — Accessories list then you will have to install this accessory from the original Windows disc. When you click on the Direct Cable Connection item you will see full instructions for running the software, using a Wizard. You need to set up the software on both computers, and you will be prompted to do this.

In the UK, a suitable parallel cable for use with Interlink or with Direct Cable Connection can be obtained from:

EQ Consultants
Allt An Fhionn,
St. Fillans,
Perthshire PH6 2NG
Scotland
Tel: (01764) 685220/685225

Other dedicated uses

The suggestions in this book have covered many of the most common ways to keep an older computer active and useful. The list is not exhaustive, and there are many other uses for an old computer. These can be put into several classes.

Time-critical actions: Some actions, such as sorting large lists or working with large spreadsheets, can take a considerable time. Though Windows allows these tasks to be done in the background while you are running another program, this has the effect of slowing down both actions because timesharing means that the processor is spending less time on each program. If one action can be carried out by the spare computer both machines can work at full speed. This is particularly useful if the machines are networked together.

Other operating systems: Your main computer is likely to make use of Windows 95 or 98, but you might want to experiment with other operating systems. Putting two operating systems into one computer is a recipe for trouble, so that using a spare machine is an attractive proposition, provided that the spare has the resources to run another operating system. You might need to expand the memory of the spare machine, though a machine that will run Windows 95 easily might not need much memory expansion to be useful for other systems.

Text only use: If your applications call for the use of both text and graphics, you might want to use a spare machine for one of these purposes, allowing the other machine to specialise. Because working with graphics requires more resources than working with text, it makes sense to use the spare machine for text. On paper, you would normally run both applications together on a single machine running Windows, but unless you are using a very fast machine you can find that both applications run rather slowly, especially if memory space is inadequate. Remember also that using more than one window, unless you use a 17 inch screen (or larger), can be awkward and time-consuming.

DIY computing hardware: Last of all, you can make use of an old machine as a form of adult Meccano set. If you have no experience of working with computer hardware this is one painless way to get some in. You might, very reasonably, not want to lift the lid on a new machine (quite apart from the risk of invalidating the warranty), but you need not feel any qualms about working on an old computer.

Remember that all the electrically dangerous parts of a computer are inside an inner box which is deliberately made

Odds and ends

difficult to take apart, so that the risks are minimal even if you work inside the main casing with the power switched on. This is the way to find out about inserting ISA cards, where the processor is placed, how to add memory and all the other tasks that are described in the book BP434 *PC hardware assistant*.

Appendices

A. Recycling computers

RecommIT is a company run by Jane Corani to recycle old computers, printer and other peripherals. No cash is paid for machines, and they are re-conditioned and sold at low prices to schools and other buyers. Typical price for a reconditioned 486 machine, complete, is around £90. *Old* laser printers sell for about the same price. RecommIT will collect for batches of 10 or more, and will clear hard drives (to MoD standards) before disposal. Companies can be provided with details of where their machines have ended up. Contact number is (01264) 355552.

Appendices

B. Batch files for MS-DOS

The normal way of using MS-DOS is to type a command and then press the ENTER key so that the computer carries out the command at once. This type of use is called **interactive**, and the alternative is called **batch** use, in which you issue a set of commands and then let the computer get on with the job of carrying out each one in sequence.

Obviously, you have to type the commands in rather a different way so that you can achieve this, because what you are doing is to write a miniature program of commands that the machine will execute later and in a particular order. This is done in MS-DOS by writing a file that is recorded on to a disc.

This type of file as used in the PC is called a batch file, and by typing the name of such a batch file, just as you type the name of a program, you can make the computer carry out, in sequence, the commands that are contained in the file. Each batch file has the extension letters of BAT, and you should not use these extension letters for any other type of file.

Suppose, for example, you created a batch file that contained instructions for copying all the files from the C:\WRITEM folder that you had modified since 1/1/1998 to a floppy in drive A. This batch file might be called BAKEMUP.BAT. The important point about such a batch file is that to carry out this action all you need to do is to place the floppy disc in the drive and type BAKEMUP, the name of the batch file, the press the RETURN key. This assumes that you have stored your batch files in a folder that is notified in the PATH command in AUTOEXEC.BAT, so that you can call up a batch file from any folder.

- Batch files provide a way of automating your work, so that you can achieve the effect of typing a number of commands by simply typing a single command, which is the name of a batch file.

Creating a batch file

A batch file, at its simplest, is a set of normal MS-DOS commands that you type and record in ASCII file codes like any other simple text. You can create batch files using Windows Notepad or with the EDIT editing program that is part of the MS-DOS system.

- You cannot prepare batch files with a word-processor unless you can set the word-processor to produce ASCII files — any other setting is likely to place unrecognisable codes into the text. Any program that is described as a text editor is suitable.

A batch file, whatever its purpose, consists of the usual commands of MS-DOS, plus a few very useful commands that are peculiar to batch files, and which make the batch file much more like a programming language in its own right. Each batch file must have the extension letters BAT, since this identifies it as a batch file when you look at the disc folder. The fact that the file has this extension also allows the machine to locate the file when you type the main filename. If you do not use the extension BAT, then the computer will treat the file like any other file of text, not as a batch file.

There is a very special reserved name for a batch file, AUTOEXEC.BAT, located in the C:\ drive. Whatever this batch file contains will be carried out automatically after the machine has read the DOS and before it is ready for you to use. Do not change this file unless you know what you are doing.

We can look now at how to construct and use a simple batch file. The batch file used as an example will make all the files in a folder called C:\TEXT into read-only form and we can call it, logically enough, RO.BAT. We start, then by running an editor such as Notepad and using the File — New command.

Appendices

Each command in the batch file needs to use a line of its own, and is typed as it would be if you were typing direct commands — in this example there is only one line to type:

    ATTRIB C:\text +R

and press the ENTER key so as to take a new line. You can then shut down the editor.

You now need to name the file and save it in the C:\ folder with the filename of RO.BAT. Once the file has been saved, it can be invoked (made to work) when you are running MS-DOS by typing RO (press RETURN key), assuming that you are using the folder in which the batch file is recorded. Saving batch files in the C:\ root folder is the easiest method of ensuring that a batch file will run no matter what folder you are using when you type the command.

- You can stop a batch file in the middle of its action by pressing the Ctrl-C keys (hold down both Ctrl and C). This brings up a message asking you to confirm that you want to stop the batch file by typing Y or N. Typing Y will stop the batch file and return you to MS-DOS. You can also use Ctrl-C to stop temporarily (perhaps to get a printer ready, for example). When you press the N key, the batch file will resume.

- You can also use the Pause key, or Ctrl-S, to halt a batch file temporarily until you press any other key. There is no option to end the batch file in this case, however.

Using ECHO

Batch files can make use of a set of commands of their own, many of which can be used only in batch files. One useful command is ECHO which exists in several forms.

@ECHO OFF will suppress the appearance of the batch file commands on the screen. Whether you use this or not is a matter of choice. Some batch file users like to see the commands appear, others do not. It is an advantage to leave the command out when you first try out a batch file, because the appearance of the commands on the screen indicate the progress of the file. Once you have tested the batch file thoroughly you can use @ECHO OFF to suppress the printing of these command lines.

ECHO has another use, to make text appear on the screen even when you have used @ECHO OFF as a first line. The text in this case is not the command lines, which remain suppressed, but any text you like to put in. For example, if your batch file contains the line:

ECHO Do you want to copy this file to A:\ ? (Y/N)

then the words of the message (but not the word ECHO) will appear when this line runs. You can use this to deliver reminders (a simple HELP system), warnings (about deleting files, for example) or error messages (about absence of parameters, for example) or any other use you can think of. You can make a batch file that consists only of ECHO lines in order to provide outline documentation for a program. You can call such a batch file from another batch file if required, using CALL followed by the name of the new batch file.

Appendices

INDEX

Index

102

Index